THE OFFICIAL AFRICAN – AMERICAN MUSEUMS AND CULTURAL GALLERIES DIRECTORY

REDEFINING AFRICAN – AMERICAN MUSEUMS

AND

COLLECTING MATERIAL FOR THE FUTURE

WILLIE E. BOX JR. AND ASSOCIATES
CHICAGO, ILLINOIS

CASS DISTRICT LIBRARY
319 M-62
CASSOPOLIS, MI 49031

THE OFFICIAL AFRICAN-AMERICAN MUSEUMS AND CULTURAL GALLERIES DIRECTORY

©1991 Willie E. Box, Jr. and Associates. All rights reserved. Printed in the United States of America. No part of this publication may be reproduced or transmitted in any form by any means, electronic or mechanical, including photocopying, recording or any information storage and retrieval system, without permission in writing from the copyright owner. For information, email: WillieBoxJr@msn.com

Willie E. Box, Jr. and Associates
WillieBoxJr@msn.com
ISBN 1-882901-38-X
Library of Congress Catalog Card Number: 93-70020

Dedication

This book is dedicated to my parents, Anna Mae Box and Willie Eugene Box, Sr., whose patience, fidelity and hard work have gone far to make this work a success.

I also would like to thank my wife, Sharon Ann Baugh-McGuire-Box, family and friends for their continued support. Once my family and friends understood what my project was about, they contributed to this book by assisting me in researching and visiting the various museums as they vacationed throughout this country.

I also want to thank W.W. Law of Savannah, Georgia who started me on this journey of researching African-American museums. It was an article in the Atlanta Constitution newspaper about Mr. Law and Cottage Museum that made me aware, that there are more African-American museums in this country, than the limited number that were being written about in the traditional museum and library organization reference books found in the public libraries and bookstores.

TABLE OF CONTENTS

PREFACE	IX-X
CHAPTER 1	1
Definition of African – American Museums.	3
Why Develop African – American Museums?	5
A Well – Kept Secret	6
CHAPTER 2	9
Alabama	11
Arizona	12
Arkansas	12
California	13
Colorado	14
Connecticut	15
Delaware	15
District of Columbia	15
Florida	17
Georgia	19
Idaho	21
Illinois	21
Indiana	22
Kansas	23
Kentucky	23
Louisiana	24
Maryland	25
Massachusetts	27
Michigan	28
Mississippi	30
Missouri	30
Nebraska	31
Nevada	31
New Jersey	32
New York	32
North Carolina	35
Ohio	36
Oklahoma	37
Pennsylvania	37
Rhode Island	38
South Carolina	38
Tennessee	39
Texas	40
Virginia	41
Washington	42
Wisconsin	42

AFRICAN-AMERICAN CANADIAN MUSEUMS
Ontario _____ 44
Nova Scotia _____ 45

CHAPTER 3 _____ 46
Individual Museum Descriptions _____ 49

CHAPTER 4 _____ 109
Historical Societies _____ 111
Genealogical Societies _____ 112
Historical Organizations _____ 114
Black Memorabilia _____ 117
Black Military History _____ 118
Associations _____ 118
Public Libraries _____ 119
Performing Groups Living History _____ 122
Film Organizations _____ 123
Traveling Museums _____ 124

CHAPTER 5 _____ 127
Uncle Remus Museum _____ 129
Harriet Beecher Stowe House & Museum _____ 129
Fort Concho _____ 129
Simpsons _____ 130
Balch Institute for Ethnic Studies _____ 131
Colonial Williamsburg's Historic Area _____ 132
Levi Coffin State Historic Site _____ 133
Delta Blues Museum _____ 133
Kentucky Derby Museum _____ 134
Thompson – Hickman Library _____ 134
Old Slave House (Crenshaw House) _____ 134
The Stagville Center _____ 135
Rankin House _____ 136
Casey Jones Railroad Museum State Park _____ 137
Savannah History Museum _____ 137
Slave Haven/Underground Railroad _____ 137

CHAPTER 6 _____ 139
Major Cities Without African – American Museums _____ 141
Secondary Cities That Need African – Americans Museums _____ 141
Africa Fact Sheet _____ 141
Carter G. Woodson – Father of African –American History _____ 143
Pledge to the Red, Black and Green _____ 144
Lift Every Voice and Sing Negro National Anthem _____ 145
Museums Books _____ 146
Magazine Articles _____ 146
Newspaper Articles _____ 147
Bibliographical Sources _____ 149
Index _____ 153

NO HISTORY

We will continue not to have a history or culture,

If it's left up to them.

You wouldn't have a museum,

If it was left up to them.

You wouldn't have a State park named after a Black leader,

If it was left up to them.

You wouldn't have a past,

If it was left up to them;

It's left up to YOU.

To build your own nation within a nation.

It is left up to YOU,

To politicize your own culture.

It is left up to YOU,

To write your own history.

It is left up to YOU,

To leave your own footprints in the sand.

It is left up to YOU!

It is left up to YOU!

It is left up to YOU!

By Willie E. Box, Jr.

PREFACE

Since 1960, African-American museums have popped up across the United States and Canada. This has added to the development and understanding of African-American and African-Canadian history and culture. These libraries, galleries, universities, private collections, and collections in cultural centers are bridging the gap that was left by historians, who had blinders on when it came to African-American history and culture. In the past, the story of our people was simply a distorted history for the glory of other ethnic groups. Now African-Americans and African-Canadians are assisting in re-writing the contributions and impact that the African community has had on North American history and European law. African artifacts and memorabilia are being collected and preserved for cultural and historical awareness.

This book is a beginning of the identification of African-American and African-Canadian museums. Through the use of these museums, the general public, along with historians, scholars, and collectors can increase and upgrade their knowledge and research of African experiences and contributions to North America and the world.

African-American museums are in the midst of re-defining the past, and developing material for future teaching situations. These museums are clearing up old myths and concepts about the role and contributions of African-American and African-Canadian history and culture.

A number of the buildings, in which these museums are housed, are stories within themselves. They express the experiences of African-Americans and African-Canadians in North America. You have old school buildings, slave quarters, courthouses, and personal property where some museums are now housed, echoing history of years past.

Prior to this book, you could only identify a few African-American museums. This book attempts to tap into a number of new resources to develop this list of museums more comprehensively. The identification of museums that have special selections or related material about the African-American and African-Canadian history and culture has also been made.

Carter G. Woodson wrote, "If a race has no history, if it has no worthwhile tradition, it becomes a negligible factor in the thought of the world, and it stands in danger of being exterminated." This book dispels the belief that African-American and African-Canadians have no history. It will also dispel the myth of racial inferiority to which the majority of Americans have subscribed.

This book was written out of a love for African-American history, and also the need to identify places where the true history of descendants from Africa could be found, and not a history told through those wearing blinders. In African-American museums across the country and in this book, you will find our story being told through our perspective and not through the lens or interpretation of others.

African-American museums are infants compared to other museums, but the subject that they construct is as ancient as man. This book attempts to introduce you to a large number of African-American and African-Canadian museums. It is the belief that no one has ever accomplished this task before. The various museums were researched and visited; this afforded a first hand look at the structure of the museums, their exhibits and artifacts. The type of museum along with their future plans were also identified.

After all these years, we've just begun to touch the tip of the ice berg of information about African American history. It is the hope of this writer that individuals will begin their research of African-American history using the information found in the number of museums provided in this book.

The challenge for the African-American museum is to develop an understanding of African-American history and culture. A role of the museum is to present this history and culture not only to America, but to the world. The museum's challenge is also to build a base from which to tell the story of a race of people who were taken from Africa, and transported across the waters to a world where they would be used for free labor. Another role of African American museums is to be committed to the concept of being an educational vehicle, revealing the history of our unique experience to the world. As an educational vehicle, the museum will not only stimulate questions covering African American history, but also offer the answers that will correct the misconceptions and beliefs used against African Americans.

Financial and or emotional support has always been a major problem for African American museums and that is a great concern. Our museums need support to provide evidence and resources that will combat the misleading information taught about Africans and African Americans. They need financial support and revenue in becoming the educational vehicle that will inform the world of the vast contributions made by Africans and their descendents. African American and African Canadian museums continue to need our support in helping them collect our wealth of information to be disseminated to the general population. It is the hope of the author that this book becomes a resource and guide for continued research into the life of Africans and African-Americans. Remember that the story of African Americans is like America, it is cracked just like the liberty bell and must be repaired, restored, rebuilt and reconstructed.

CHAPTER 1

"There is no sense in hate; it comes back to you; therefore, make your history so laudable, magnificent and untarnished, that another generation will not seek to repay your seeds for the sins inflicted upon their fathers. The bones of injustice have a peculiar way of rising from the tombs to plague and mock the iniquitous."

Marcus Garvey

DEFINITION OF AFRICAN-AMERICAN MUSEUMS
AND THE REASONS FOR THEIR EXISTENCE

The word museum comes from the Greek word *mouseion*. In ancient Greece, the *mouseion* was the temple of Muses, the goddess of arts and sciences. During the second century B.C., the word was used for a library and research area in Alexandria, Egypt. Webster's dictionary defines a museum as a building or rooms where a collection of objects illustrating science, ancient life, art, history, or other items are kept and displayed. Museums are also defined as buildings or places where works of art or other objects of permanent value are kept and displayed.

Today when you say African-American museums, you are using a very loose form of the term museum. According to the following organizations, The American Association of Museums, The American Association for State and Local History, and The International Council of Museums subscribe to a set of standards in which museums can be accredited and defined. Some of those standards are as follows:

- Have the financial resources sufficient to operate effectively
- Have a full time director to whom authority is delegated for day-to-day operations
- Have at least one paid professional staff with museum knowledge and experience
- Have a formal and appropriate program of documentation, care, and use of collections
- Use and interpret objects and/or a site for the public presentation of regularly scheduled programs and exhibits

It has come to the attention of this writer that a large majority of our African-American museums lack most of the standards needed to become accredited, recognized or defined by the previously mentioned mainstream museum associations. The aforementioned is due in part to a lack of funding and a limited pool of trained personnel from which to hire. When it comes to securing staff, documenting materials, scheduling exhibits and collections, and preserving knowledgeable boards of directors to develop the broad goals of museum programming, you find that there are only a few people qualified or willing to accept such responsibilities. It may take triple the time and financial resource for most African-American museums to open their doors, compared to their White counter parts. Most buildings that now house some of our African American museums required unforeseen major renovations prior to taking occupancy. These unexpected costs put a strain on already limited resources and therefore caused lengthy delays while attempts were made to procure additional funding. As the delays and time marched on, inflation of the price of material and labor seeped into the total cost of the project, therefore creating a cycle of constantly needing to raise additional funds to complete the renovations.

If we use the above mentioned definition of a museum, only five percent of the African-American museums in the country would fulfill their definition. This is the reason why only a few selected African American museums are listed in prominent directories of museums.

What is an African-American museum, and how is it defined through the lens of an African-American? We see museums, as do most, as repositories of history and cultural artifacts. Our African-American museums have several purposes and reasons for their existence, some being to collect, preserve, teach, exhibit, and interpret history and artifacts to the community. Another reason for the existence of African-American museums is to inform the public of its presence within and outside of their neighborhoods. But, a major reason for the presence of the museums that would set them apart from the mainstream museum, is to belie western thought as it refers to the history of African-Americans.

In defining African-American museums, we must look at the following: why there needs to be museums featuring the history of descendants from Africa; the various types of museums; why these museums are a well-kept secret; why they must move beyond the history of African-Americans; and what these museums should focus on to prepare themselves to be a viable entity for the future.

They exist to make people aware of the rich history and contributions made by Africans. If we, along with our African-American museums do not honor and preserve our past, we will dishonor our present and our future. It is well known that the history of the African is the oldest history on this earth, but is the least publicized of all races. The continuous probing and studying of our past by anthropologists and archaeologists indicate that Central Africa bears evidence of indeed being the location of the first humans on earth, but this fact meets with resistance and opposition from many. Museums and historians have covered up, hidden, and twisted our history to fit their purposes. The continent of Africa has also revealed the oldest human-like fossils found to date. Civilization started in Africa and moved down the Nile River. Discoveries have led to the finding of the oldest human fossils in Africa. Donald Johanson and Tom Gray, on the 30th of November, 1974 at the site of Hadar in Ethiopia, found the skeleton of what later became known as Lucy, which is dated to just less than 3.18 million years old.

The second reason for the existence of African-Americans museums is to refute Western thoughts that misrepresent the African and African-American experience. The museums must question and challenge the belief system of Western philosophy that has attempted to destroy African and African- American people and their place in history.

African-American museums must be created to preserve the truth about the development and history of the Egyptian-African origin that preceded the history of Greece or Rome. Our museums must negate the Western belief that the origin of Egyptian-Africans came from Western civilization, which was in Greece and Rome. We must emphatically deny that concept of African civilization growing out of Western culture and boldly proclaim the opposite that Western civilization grew out of African origins.

Another reason for the existence of the African-American museum is to assist in freeing minds from a mental bondage that has affected thinking of many as it relates to African and African-American history. Asa Hilliard refers to this mental bondage as "a failure to challenge beliefs and patterns of thought which control man but man will defend and protect those beliefs and patterns of thought virtually with his last dying breath." So it is this mental bondage that must be changed with the assistance of African-American museums.

It is the role of African-American museums to defy the beliefs and thought patterns of the Western civilization. The mission of the museums is to challenge individuals to stop readily accepting information given by the creators of these systems that continue to practice and teach people misrepresented beliefs. Some of us have become dependent on these doctrines of convictions. Through the African – American museums, the new African and African-American scholars now have a platform to express new treatments of thought, and challenge old bedrock beliefs and doctrines. It is through African-American museums that the impetus of change can take place. Today's historians now have the opportunity to interpret history with the assistance of African-American museums. Our museums and historians will be able to provide accurate interpretations of historical events. This may persuade those who have methodically excluded us to change their outlook on the contributions made by people of African descent.

The museums' mission is also to address the heritage of those who live or were born in America, but whose ancestors were from Africa. The focus of African-American museums is to assist in developing the link between African-Americans and Africans. African-American museums must take pride in our rich birthright and preserve the culture for future generations. There is a need for focusing on the link between the African and African-American history by acknowledging that relationship and glorifying those past roots.

A further reason for African-American museums to exist is to teach our history and develop material that could be used to prove misleading material presented by those who wish to discredit the history of descendants from Africa to be false. Our museums would partner with others to instruct and equip teachers to prepare lessons in all areas of African-American history, culture and life. African-

American historians such as William E. B. DuBois, Carter G. Woodson, and Charles Wesley, all earned doctorates, examined, interpreted, and wrote the role of African Americans in history. They reinterpreted the racist bias against African-Americans that was defined by the White historians from the Dunning-Burgess Phillips School. That is why African-American museums must take up the challenge to continue to educate people and develop teachers to have the where-with-all and accurate information to tell our true story and not allow others to falsly interpret our past.

The final reason for the presence of African-American museums is to regularly schedule and display exhibits that mirror the past, present and future of African-Americans and to interpret the meaning of those facts to the general public. Each year, more African-Americans learn about their heritage through the exhibits and newly formed programs presented at our African American museums.

WHY DEVELOP AFRICAN-AMERICAN MUSEUMS?

There is a need to understand the history of our race and culture. The African-American has not been adequately represented in this country's history. We are faced with the challenge of building a historical base to tell our story and an agency from which to tell it. African-American museums must be committed to the concept of being an educational vehicle, revealing the history of our unique experience to all. This educational vehicle will stimulate questions focusing on African-American history; the museums will also provide the factual answers.

Who are the African-American pioneers, inventors, revolutionaries, cowboys? Was DuSable the first settler in the territory that later would be known as the city of Chicago? Was Fort Del Mose in Florida the first all black town? These are only a few of the many questions that have been asked over the years by African-Americans, but without a reference from where to locate the answers. With the continuous interpretation that African-Americans didn't assist in this country's development, or lacked the knowledge to invent, the history and accomplishments of African-Americans are misinterpreted and misrepresented.

Malcolm X told us that, "Just as a tree without roots is dead, a people without history or cultural roots also become a dead people. And when you look at us, those of us who call ourselves Negro, we are like a dead people. We have nothing to identify ourselves as part of the human family." That is why African-Americans must not leave it up to others to research, collect, preserve and share our rich heritage. African-Americans working with our museums must "take point" and lead our communities to become enlightened to the true history or our people. Our museums must assist us in telling our own stories and singing our own praises.

TYPES OF MUSEUMS

A survey conducted for the National Conference of State Museums Association in 1998 attempted to count the number of museums in the U.S. and Canada. The survey estimated a number of 15,848 museums. The second effort was the database complied by the Institute of Museum and Library Services. This database contained 15,460 organizations in the United States and Canada, ranging from private, state, university, local foundations, federal, county, and church operated. Over two hundred and seventy African-American and African-Canadian museums have been identified in this book, with only a handful officially registered with the African-American Museum Association or American Association of Museums. This has not stopped these organizations from functioning as museums, libraries, archives, cultural centers, galleries, historical societies or historical sites. What's more important are the purposes for which they are open and the content of material that is displayed within their buildings for the general public. In the United States and Canada, there are three main types of museums: art, history and science/technological. The majority of African-American museums can be categorized as either art or history. Only one can be listed under science/technology, which is the *I.P. Stanback Museum and*

Planetarium at South Carolina State College (founded in April 1980). This absence of African-American museums focusing on science/technology should to be addressed, because there have been significant accomplishments made by African-Americans in science and technology. For instance, George Washington Carver, Daniel Hale Williams, and many others need their stories of science and medicine repeatedly told.

There should be specialty museums that focus on the military, oral history, children's activities, aviation, medicine, maritime, radio/television, African colonies, slave forts, and newspaper. These are just a few of the specialty museums needed to promote the rich contributions of African Americans. We need museums to interpret the Constitution, Declaration of Independence, Emancipation Proclamation, Morrill Act and other documents through the eyes of African-Americans. We need to examine law cases such as Dred Scott v. Sanford, Brown v. the Board of Education, McCabe v. the Atchison Topeka and Santa Fe Railway Company, Plessy v. Ferguson, Sweat v. Plainer, Guinn v. United States, Nixon v. Herndon, Grovey v. Townsend, Smith v. Allwright, Shelley v. Kramer, Mitchell v. United States.

What do these museums collect? Each collection varies. Some museums specialize in certain subjects or themes. The Black Fashion Museum in New York collects garments exclusively designed by African-Americans. The Philadelphia Doll Museum collects African-American dolls. The National Civil Rights Museum of Memphis Tennessee and the Ralph Mark Gilbert Civil Rights Museum of Savannah Georgia are civil rights museums focusing on the struggle made during the Civil Rights Era. In Alabama, the W.C. Handy Cabin and Museum focuses on his musical works. Some museums focus only on a single person. Other museums display wax figures of famous persons. But in general, the museums collect such items as paintings, etchings, prints, wood, cloth, paper sculpture, ceramic, glass, textiles (costumes/clothing), jewelry, photographs, motion pictures, tools and equipment, toys, dolls, books, manuscripts, maps, weapons, stamps, musical instruments, etc.

Some of the African-American museums are located in metropolitan areas or cities. Eighty percent of the museums are east of the Mississippi River, and more than half are in the northeast area of the country. The majority of African-American people are now living in urban areas. African-Americans are the first group that needs to be aware of the contributions of their race. African-Americans must be aware that they are a valued people with a great deal of worth. They must know that their race has accomplished a great many things.

African-Americans must have culturally relevant teachings in a more controlled nurturing environment. More African-American museums are needed in our urban communities with expansion to the suburbs and later an out-stretch to rural areas of the country. African-American museums must feed the belly, and this will in turn develop the mind. They must branch out to all areas in developing African- American themes. Our museums must feed us until our bellies are full of the wealth of our African heritage.

A WELL-KEPT SECRET

African-American museums have experienced growth across the country over the last 40 years. Unfortunately, they have also become a well-kept secret outside of the Black community (and even within the community). With increased awareness of culture and history, African-American museums were looked at with racist attitudes and eyes. Decendants from Africa, who would benefit the most, did not understand the depth of the camouflage used to bury African-Americans true history.

Over the past 40 years, there has been a continued emergence of African American museums. The growth has been slow but steady. Publicizing African American museums has been an enormous task. There is a continuous need to inform the public of their presence and role. After 40 years, African-American museums are still a will kept secret in the communities they serve. We go back to one of the roles of the African-American museum and that is to ensure that their public is aware of its existence.

African-American museums have been piecing together our history and missing the target when it comes to resources for materials to study in order to learn more of ourselves. It is the intention of this book to provide a source for novices and serious students of this field. Continued research and study should lead to a more sober action in the further development of African-American museums. This will allow African-American students to have a place to further develop skills, gain knowledge, and to more accurately interpret history.

Now is the time for African-Americans to start looking at their history, relating it to present experiences, and celebrating them all. No, this does not mean a celebration with alcohol and/or drugs, but with a sense of soberness, motivation, and intellectual drive. We have to look beyond the small area of urban cities and influence the countryside where our great-great grandparents lived prior to our migration into the urban conclaves. We must reach out to the heartland with museums glorifying our history and uncovering the well kept secret of our past.

It should be the decision of African-Americans to interpret the meaning of their history. We must take the initiative to determine what is taught and written about our experiences in history and the present. We must ensure that our ancestors are not dehumanized and their true actions and deeds are recorded in an accurate and appropriate manner. Honor must be given to the shedding of their blood, the sweat on their brows, and the falling of many tears from their eyes. All must be made aware that our history has meaning for both the living and dead. So that there is hope for the future, even the unborn child must know upon birth, that he/she indeed has a rich history,. It is only through us that the first slave can reach the finish line.

There is a new battleground emerging, which is the redefinition of African history. And, with this new confrontation African-American museums must take the lead in the fight. Without placing historical events of the continent at the center, you can't really focus clearly on anything that African American people have done in the United States. Our history started before slavery; it started with the first man on earth, who was found in Africa.

WHAT SHOULD BE DONE IN BUILDING FOR THE FUTURE?

There are several actions we as a people in concert with our African-American museums must take as we forge into the future and they are as follows:

- Ensure that accurate information of the heritage of Africans and African-Americans is present in textbooks that are use in our schools
- Prepare teachers to instruct their elementary, high school and college students on the history, accomplishments, and struggle of Africans and African-Americans
- Expand individuals knowledge of the accomplishments and struggles of our African-American people
- Continue to accurately write our history. Paraphrasing what Cicero once wrote; people without a written history are a people destined to remain in the infancy of civilization. The story of African-Americans is not a story of a young child, but that of an old man.
- Demand that our history not be written in an inferior, dehumanizing manor, but with great respect of our accomplishments and struggle
- View the history and experience of Africans and African-Americans through a different lens. The truth is the lens of knowledge of our past experiences which should guide us into the future. We must build on the past and move forward from the holocaust condition from which African-American people have survived.
- Have African-American historians along with African-American museum redefine our heritage. African-American museums must be a vital force in shaping the past and future interpretation of African-American history. Telling the story of our people is the main goal of the African-American museums.

CHAPTER 2

African-American Name Change: Negative and Positive
If you are going to call me Black, use a capital "B"

Alabama

Birmingham

    Birmingham Civil Rights Institute
520 – 16th Street N.
Birmingham 35203 (Toll Free) 1-(866) 328-9696 (205) 328-9696

    Alabama Jazz Hall of Fame Museum
1631 4th Ave. North
Birmingham 36203 (205) 254-2731

Florence

    W.C. Handy Cabin and Museum
620 West College Street
Florence 35630 (205) 760-6434
Director - Barbara Broach   Founded - 1968

Gadsden

    Luv Life Collectibles and Living History Museum
1136 – 7th Ave.
Gadsden 35901   (256) 549-1534

Huntsville

    Black Historical Arts Museum
320 Church Street Northwest
Huntsville 35801   (256) 539-0080

Mobile

    Bishop State Black History Museum
Central Campus
1365 Martin Luther King Jr. Ave.
Mobile 36603-5362 (251) 405 - 4457

    Mobile Black History Museum
269 N. Broad Street
Mobile 36603-5800

    National African – American Archives and Museum
564 Dr. M.L. King Jr. Avenue
Mobile 36603 (251) 433 – 8511 Fax (251) 461-4443

    National African American Archives
905 Government Street
Mobile 36604   (251) 433- 4265

Montgomery

    Rosa Parks Library & Museum
251 Montgomery Street
Montgomery 36104   (334) 241-8661
Web – tsum.edu/museum   Type of Museum – History
Director – Georgette M. Norman   Founded – December 1, 2000

Normal

Alabama State Black Archives Research Center and Museum
P.O. Box 595
Normal 35762 (256) 372-5846 Fax (256) 372-5338
Web - archivemuseumcenter.mus.al.us
E-Mail – archivemuseumcenter@aamu.edu
Type of Museum – History
Director - Dr. James W. Johnson   Founded -1990

Tuscaloosa

Murphy African – American Museum
2601 Bryant Drive
Tuscaloosa 35401 (205) 758 – 2861   (205) 758 – 2238

Tuskegee

Commodores Museum
208 Martin Luther King Hwy
Tuskegee 36086 (334) 724-0777

Tuskegee Institute National Historic Site
1212 Old Montgomery Road
Tuskegee 36888 (205) 727-6390
Director: Jerry Belson   Founded 1941

George Washington Carver Museum
1212 Old Montgomery Road
Tuskegee 36088 (205) 727-6390
Founded 1941

Wetumpka

The Elmore County Association of Black Heritage Museum of Black History
1004 Lancaster Street
Wetumpka 36092 (334) 567- 5330   (334) 567-1304
Type of Museum - History
Director – Gwen Turner   Founded – 1986

ARIZONA

Phoenix

George Washington Carver Museum and Culture Center
415 E. Grant St.
Phoenix 85004   (602) 254-7516

ARKANSAS

Little Rock

EMOBA – The Museum of Black Arkansans
1208 Louisiana Street
Little Rock 72214   (501) 372-0018

Old Washington
>The Ethnic Minorities Memorabilia Association
>Franklin Street   P.O. Box 55
>Old Washington 71862-0055   (870) 983-2482

Pine Bluff
>Leedell Moorehead – Graham Fine Arts Gallery
>University of Arkansas at Pine Bluff
>1200 North University Ave.
>Pine Bluff 71601 (870) 575- 8236 Fax (870) 543-8232
>Type of Museum – Art & History
>Director – Ruth Pasquine   Founded – 1965

CALIFORNIA

Allensworth
>Colonel Allen Allensworth State Historic Park
>Star Route 1
>Allensworth 93219 (805) 849 - 3433

Fresno
>African American Museum
>1857 Fulton Street
>Fresno 93721   (559) 268-7102

Lancaster
>Antelope Valley African American Museum
>416 W. Lumber Street
>Lancaster 93534   (661) 723-0811

Los Angeles
>African American Firefighter Museum
>1401 S. Central Ave.
>Los Angeles 90021 (213) 744-1730 Fax (213) 744-1731
>Web afr.org/aafm.htm   E-Mail aaffmuseum@aol.com
>Type of Museum – History
>Director - Brent Burton   Founded - December 13, 1997
>
>Brockman Gallery
>4334 DeGnan Boulevard
>Los Angeles 90008 (213) 294-3766
>Director: Alonzo Davis
>
>California Afro-American Museum Exposition Park
>600 State Drive
>Los Angeles 90037 (213) 744-7432   Fax (213) 744-2050
>Web – caam.ca.gov   E-Mail – derippens@caamuseum.org
>Founded – 1977   Director – David Crippens
>Type of Museum – History Established by State of California

Dunbar Hotel Cultural and Historical Museum
4225 South Central Avenue
Los Angeles 90011 (213) 678-6628
Founded 1974, Reopened 1989

Museum of African-American Art
4006 Crenshaw Boulevard - 3rd Floor
Los Angeles 90008 (323) 294-7071
Director - Mary Jane Hewitt   Founded - 1976

Oakland

Northern California Center for Afro-American History
5606 San Pablo Avenue
Oakland 94608 (415) 658-3158
Founded 1985 (as the East Bay Negro
Historical Society)

Ebony Museum of Art
1034 14th Street
Oakland 91612 (415) 763-0141
Director - Assa Touri Bernita   Founded June 1980

Perris

Dora Nelson African American History Museum
316 E. 7th Street
 Perris 92570   (909) 657-6032

San Diego

African American Museum of Fine Arts
3025 Fir Street
San Diego 92102   (619) 696-7799
www.aamfa.org

San Francisco

San Francisco African-American Historical and Cultural Society, Inc.
Fort Mason Center Building C, Room 165
San Francisco 94123   (415) 441-0640
E-Mail – sfaahcs@fast-mail.org
Type of Museum – History, Art, Library & Cultural
Director – William Hoskins   Founded – 1955

COLORADO

Denver

Black American West Museum and Heritage Center
3091 California Street
Denver 80205 (303) 292- 2566 Fax (303) 382- 1981
Web - Coax.net/people/lwf/bawmus.htm
Type of Museum - History
Founded - 1974

Stiles African American Heritage Center
2607 Glenarm Place
Denver 80205 (303) 294- 0597 Fax (303) 388- 9121
Type of Museum – History
Director – Grace Stiles   Founded – 1998

CONNECTICUT

New Haven

Connecticut Afro-American Historical Society, Inc.
444 Orchard Street
New Haven 06511 (203) 776-4907
Founded - February 1971

DELAWARE

Wilmington D. C.

Afro-American Historical Society of Delaware
512 East 4th Street
Wilmington 19801 (302) 984-1423 (302) 984-1420
Founded - May 1986

DISTRICT OF COLUMBIA

Washington

Black Fashion Museum
2007 Vermont Ave. N.W.
Washington 20001 (202) 667- 0744   Fax – (202) 667-4379
Web- bfmdc.org   E-Mail – bfmdc@aol.com
Type of Museum – Cultural
Director – Joyce Bailey   Founded - 1979

Afro-American Doll Gallery
1794 Verbena Street N.W.
Washington, D.C. 20012 (202) 829-7170
Director - Erlene Reed

African Studies and Research Program
Howard University
P.O. Box 231
Washington, D.C. 20059 (202) 636-7115
Director - Dr. Robert J. Cummings   Founded - 1954

Anacostia Museum Smithsonian Institution
1901 Fort Place S.E.
Washington, D.C. 20020 (202) 287-3306
Director - John Kinard   Founded - September 1967

Evans-Tibbs Collection
1910 Vermont Avenue N.W.
Washington, D.C. 20001 (202) 234-8164
Director - Thurlow E. Tibbs, Jr.   Founded - May 1978

Frederick Douglass Home
1411 West Street S.E.
Washington, D.C. 20020 (202) 426-5960   Fax - (202) 426-0880
E – Mail – Nps. Gov\ frdo
Type of Museum – Historic House
Site Manager - Derrick Cook   Founded - 1916

Gallery of Art
Howard University
2455 Sixth Street N.W.
Washington, D.C. 20059 (202) 636-7047
Director - Winston Kennedy   Founded - 1928

Moorland-Spingarn Research Center
Howard University
Washington, D.C. 20059 (202) 636-7239
Director - Thomas C. Battle   Founded - 1973

National Museum of African Art Smithsonian Institution
950 Independence Avenue S.W.
Washington, D.C. 20560 (202) 357-4600
Director - Sylvia Williams   Founded - 1964; renamed 1981

Tomorrow's World Art Center
P.O. Box 56197
Washington, D.C. 20011 (202) 829-1188
Director - Georgette Powell   Founded - 1975

Bethune Museum and Archives, Inc.
1318 Vermont Avenue N.W.
Washington, D.C. 20005 (202) 332-1233   (202) 332-9201
Founded - November 1979

Carter G. Woodson Center
1401 14th Street N.W.
Washington, D.C. 20005 (202) 667-2822
Executive Director - J.Rupert Scott

National Council for Education and Economic Development
P.O. Box 7067
Washington, D.C. 20024 (202) 667-6444
Director - Tom Mack

FLORIDA

Bradenton
Manatee Family Heritage House
5840 26th Street West
Bradenton 34207 (941) 752-5319

Clearwater
Dorothy Thompson African-American Museum
1501 Madison Avenue North
Clearwater 33755-2638
(813) 447-1037

Crestview
Carver-Hill Memorial Museum Fairview Park
900 McClelland Street
Crestview 32536-3449 (850) 682-4003 Fax (850) 682-3449
Type of Museum – History Director – Caroline J. Allen Founded – May 1975

Daytona Beach
Carl Swisher Library/Learning Resource Center
Bethune-Cookman College
640 - 2nd Avenue
Daytona Beach 32115 (904) 255-1401 Ext.372
Founded - 1971

Deland
African American Museum of the Art
325 South Clara Ave.
P.O. Box 1319
Deland 32721 –1319   (386) 736-4004   Fax (386) 736-4088
Web- africanmuseumdeland.org   E-Mail – art@africanamerica
Type of Museum – Art
Director – Irene Johnson   Founded - 1994

Eatonville
Zora Neale Hurston Museum of Art
227 East Kennedy Boulevard
Mailing Address: P.O. Box 2586
Eatonville 32751-5303 (407) 647-3307

Fort Lauderdale
Old Dillard High School Museum
1009 N.W. 4th Street
Fort Lauderdale 33311 (945) 765 – 6952 Fax (945) 765-8899
E-Mail – maattchet@hotmail.com Curator – Ernestine Ray   Founded – 1993
Type of Museum – Local History & Historic House

Key West

Lofton B. Sands African Bahamas Museum
324 Truman
Key West 33040 (305) 295 - 7337

Miami

Antigua Gallery, Inc.
5138 Biscayne Boulevard
Miami 33137 (305) 447-4950 (305) 759-5355
Director - Caleb A. Davis   Founded - 1984

Black Heritage Museum
Miracle Center Mall
3301 Coral Way
Coral Gables
P.O. Box 570327
Miami 33257-0327 (305) 252-3535 Founded - 1988

Black Heritage Museum
(Gulf Stream Elementary School)
20900 SW 97th Avenue
Miami 33257   (305) 252-3535

Joseph Caleb Community Center
5400 N.W. 22nd Avenue
Miami 33142   (305) 638-6064

Black Archives History and Research Foundation
Of Southern Florida
5400 N.W. 22nd Avenue-Suite 702
Miami 33142   (305) 638-6064

Chapman House
1200 N.W. 6th Avenue
Miami 33136-2409

Orlando

Well's Built Museum of African American History
511 West South Street
Orlando 32801 (407) 245- 7535

Pensacola

Julee Cottage Museum
210 E. Zaragoza Street
Pensacola 32501

Tallahassee

Black Archives Research Center and Museum
Florida A&M University
P.O. Box 809
Tallahassee 32307   (904) 559-3020
Director - James Eaton   Founded - 1971

Tampa

Museum of African-American Art
1308 North Marion Street
Tampa 33602-2917 (813) 272-2466

Florida Great Blacks in Wax
220 East Madison Street
Tampa 33602 (813) 226- 2424

White Springs

Stephen Foster State Folk
Culture Center
U.S. Highway 41 North
White Springs 32096 (904) 397-2733

GEORGIA

Albany

Albany Civil Rights Movement Museum at Old Mt. Zion Church
326 Whitney Street
P.O. Box 6036
Albany 31706   (912) 432-1698   Fax (912) 432-2150

Atlanta

African-American Family History Assn., Inc.
P.O. Box 115268
Atlanta 30310   (404) 346-1084
President - JoAnne Martin   Founded - 1977

APEX (Afro-American Panoramic Experience)
Collection of Life and Heritage, Inc.
135 Auburn Avenue N.E.
Atlanta 30303   (404) 523-2739   Fax (404) 523-3248
Web – apexmusuem.org   E-Mail – apexmuseum@aol.com
Type of Museum – History - Director – Dan Moore   Founded - July 1978

Collections of Life and Heritage
171 Ashby Street S.W.
Atlanta 30314   (404) 758-5308   Director - Dan Moore

Herndon Home
587 University Place N.W.
Atlanta 30314 (404) 581-9813   Fax (404) 588-0239
Web – Herndonhome.org   E-Mail – info@herndonhome.org
Type of Museum - Historic House Director - Carole Merritt   Founded - 1983

Martin Luther King Library and Archives
King Center for Non-Violent Social Change
450 Auburn Avenue N.E.
Atlanta 30312   (404) 524-1956 Director - Louise Cook   Founded - 1968

Ruth Hodges Gallery
Morris Brown College
6213 M.L.King Drive S.W.
Atlanta 30314   (404) 525-7831 Ext. 246
Director - Dr. Leransaw   Founded - 1976

Waddell Gallery
Atlanta University
Chestnut Street, S.W.
Atlanta 30314 (404) 681-0251

Hammond's House
503 Peeples Street S.W.
Atlanta 30312 (404) 752-8730

Augusta

Lucy Craft Laney Museum of Black History
1116 Phillips Street
Augusta 30901 (706) 724 - 3576   Fax (706) 724-357
Web – Lucycraftlaneymuseum.com
E-Mail - lolmuseum@4tscomputers.com
Type of Museum – Art, Historic House & History
Director - James A. Young III   Founded - 1991

Cartersville

Noble Hill Black History Museum
2371 Joe Frank Harris Pkwy.
Cartersville 30120-4605 (404) 382-3392

Columbus

Art 'N Artifacts Gallery
531 First Avenue
Columbus 31901-3103 (404) 324-7706
Director - Judith Grant Shabazz

Macon

Harriet Tubman Historical and Cultural Museum
340 Walnut Street
P.O. Box 6671
Macon 31201 (478) 743- 8544 Fax (478) 743- 9063
Web – Tubmanmuseum.com   President and Founder - Father Richard C. Keil
E-Mail - Tubmanmuseum@tubmanmuseum.com
Type of Museum – History, Art & Cultural Founded - August 1982

Madison

Morgan County African American Museum
156 Academy Street
Madison 30650 (706) 342-9191

Savannah

King – Tisdell Cottage
502 East Harris Street
Savannah 31401 (912) 234 – 8000 Fax (912) 234 – 8001   Type of Museum - Art
Web – Kingtisdell.org   E – Mail Kingisdell@bellsouth.net

Ralph Mark Gilbert Civil Rights Museum
460 Martin Luther King Jr. Blvd.
Savannah 31401 (912) 231 – 8900 Fax (912) 234-2577
Web - Savannahcivilrightsmuseum.com
Type of Museum – History
Director - Helen Johnson   Founded - September 1999

Idaho

Boise
Idaho Black History Museum
Julia Davis Park
508 N. Julia Drive
Boise 83702 (208) 433-0017 Fax (208) 433- 0048
E-Mail – ibhm2mindspring.com
Type of Museum – Historic House
Director – Kimetha Coleman   Founded – March 3, 1999

Illinois

Aurora

African – American Heritage and Black Veterans Archives
126 S. Kendall Street
Aurora 60505-4530 (630) 897 – 5581   (800) 477-4369

Champaign

Hot House Gallery
118½ North Neil   {closed}
Champaign 61821   (217) 356-9256
Director: Scotland C. Brown   Founded November 1987

Chicago

Ancient Egyptian Museum and Institute
3849 South Michigan Avenue   {closed}
Chicago 60653 (312) 268-3700 or 363-4128
Director - Walter Williams

Bronzeville Children's Museum   (future site)
95th and Western Ave.
Evergreen Park 60805 (708) 636 – 9504

Chess Records Museum
2120 S. Michigan Ave.
Chicago 60616-1713 (312) 808-1286

Phillip Randolph Pullman Porter Museum
10406 South Maryland Ave.
Chicago 60680 –6276   (773) 928-3935

DuSable Museum of African-Amercian History
740 East 56th Place
Chicago 60637 (773) 947-0600
Type of Museum – History Founded 1961

Malcolm X College
1900 West Van Buren Street
Chicago 60612 (312) 850- 7000

Southside Community Art Center
3831 South Michigan Avenue
Chicago 60653 (773) 373-1026
Type of Museum -Art
Director - Gerald Sanders Founded - 1940 (W.P.A.)

> Sole survivor of nearly 100 neighborhood art centers established under the Depression Works Progress Administration.

Decatur

African American Cultural and Genealogical Society of
Illinois Museum
314 N. Main Street
Decatur 62523   (217) 429 - 7458 Fax (217) 429 – 7861
Web - African American Cultural. Org   E-Mail aacgs@springnet1.com
Type of Museum – History, Library & Cultural Center
Director - Evelyn Hood   Founded - August 31, 1993

East St. Louis

Katherine Dunham Museum
1005 Pennsylvania Ave.
East St. Louis 62201   (618) 271-3367 Fax (618) 874-6480
Director- Jennelle Stovall

Peoria

Downstate Afro-American Hall of Fame Museum
309 South DuSable
Peoria 61605   (309) 688-3667

INDIANA

Evansville

Evansville African American Museum
579 Lincoln Avenue
Evansville 47731-3124 (812) 423-5188   Fax (812) 423-3787
E-Mail – eaamuseum@aol.com

Indianapolis

Madame C.J. Walker Theatre Center & Museum
617 Indiana Avenue
Indianapolis 46202   (317) 236-2099 Fax (317) 236- 2097
E-Mail – Mmewalker.org
Type of Museum – History, Cultural & Memorabilia
Director – Cynthia Holmes – Garner Founded - 1979   Museum - 1997

Crispus Attucks Museum
1140 Dr. Martin Luther King Jr. Street
Indianapolis 46202   (317) 226 – 2430   Fax (317) 226-4611
www.crispusattucksmuseum.ips.k12.in.us
E-mail Taylorg@mail.ips.k12.in.us

KANSAS

Wichita

First National Black Historical Society of Kansas
601 North Water
P.O. Box 2695
Wichita 67201   (316) 262-7651   Fax (316) 683-1247
Director - Founded - November 1973

Levenworth

Afro-American Historical Society
P.O. Box 3151
834 Pottawatumie Street
Levenworth 66048   (913) 651-4584
Director - Georgia Hester   Founded – 1984

KENTUCKY

Franklin   African American Heritage Center
500 Jefferson Street
P.O. Box 353
Franklin 42135 (270) 586-0099

Hickman

Warren Thomas Black Museum
603 Moulton Street
Thomas Chapel CME Church
Hickman 42050 - Built in 1890 by ex-slaves

Louisville

Kentucky Center for African American Heritage
433 South 18th Street.
Louisville 40203 (502) 583 – 4100   Fax (502) 583 – 4112

Maysville

National Underground Railroad Museum
115 East Third Street
Maysville 41056 (606) 783- 2668

LOUISIANA

Alexandria

        Arna Bontemps African American Museum and Cultural Center
        1327 Third Street
        Alexandria 71301   (318) 473 – 4692   Fax (318) 473-4675
        E-Mail arnabont@bellsouth.net Web- arnobontempsmuseum.com
        Type of Museum – Historic Director – Gwendolyn Elmore - Founded – 1988

Donaldsonville

        River Road African American Museum
        406 Charles Street
        Donaldsonville 70346   (225) 473-4814   Fax (225) 647-5711
        Web – africanamericanmuseum.org   E-Mail – aamuseum@bellsouth.net
        Type of Museum – History, Art, Cultural & Historic House
        Director – Kathe Hamlorick   Founded – March 1994

Monroe

        Northwest Louisiana Delta African American Heritage Museum
        503 Plum St.
        Monroe 71210-0168 (318) 323-1167

New Orleans

        Amistad Research Center Library/Archives
        Tulane University
        6823 St. Charles Ave.
        New Orleans 70118   (504) 865-5535
        Amistadresearchcenter.org
        Director - Clifton Johnson Founded - September 1966
        (Archives and library at Fisk University moved to Tulane University)

        Black Arts National Diaspora Museum
        1530 N. Claiborne
        New Orleans 70116-1340 (504) 949-2263

        Louisiana Museum of African American History
        1210 Governor Nicholls St.
        New Orleans 70116

        Musee Rosette Rochon
        1515 Pauger Street
        (By Appointment Only)
        New Orleans 70116 (504) 947–7673
        Type of Museum – Historic House
        Director – Don G. Richmond Founded – 1998

        New Orleans African American Museum
        Of Art, Culture and History
        1418 Governor Nicholls Street
        New Orleans 70116 (504) 319-5415
        Web www.noaam.org

Shreveport

Stephens African – American Museum
2810 Lindholm
Shreveport 71109 (318) 635-2147

MARYLAND

Annapolis

Banneker-Douglass Museum of Afro-American Life and History
84 Franklin Street
Annapolis 21401 (410) 216-6180 Founded - 1984
Web – www. marylandhistoricaltrust.net/bdm.html

Baltimore

Beulah M. Davis Special Collection
Morgan State University
1700 E. Coldspring Lane
Baltimore 21209 (443) 885-3458 Fax (443) 885-8246
Web- www.Library.Morgan.edu
Type of Museum – Library Director – Karen Robertson Founded -1926

Black American Museum
1769 Carswell Street
Baltimore 21218 (410) 243-9600
Director - Frank Richardson Founded - 1968

The Cab Calloway Jazz Institute
Coppin State College
Parlette L. Moore Library
2500 West North Avenue
Baltimore 21216 Web – www.copin.edu
(410) 333-5926 Fax (301) 333-7370 Founded -1985

The Eubie Blake National Institute Museum and Cultural Center
847 N. Howard
Baltimore 21201 (410) 225-3130 Founded 1978
Web – www.eubie.org

Morgan State University
Gallery of Art
Hillen & Coldspring Lane
Baltimore 21239 (410) 444-3030
Director - James Lewis Founded - 1952

Great Blacks in Wax Museum
1601 East North Avenue
Baltimore 21213 (410) 563-3404 Fax (410) 675-5040
Web – greatblacksinwax.org Type of Museum – History & Wax Founded - 1983
E- Mail – spoteat@greatblacksinwax.org

Lillie Carroll Jackson Museum, Inc.
Civil Rights Museum
1320 Eutaw Place
Baltimore 21217   (410) 783-5469

NAACP/ Henry Lee Moon Library and National Civil Rights Archives
4805 Mt. Hope Drive
Baltimore 21215-3206 (410) 358 – 8900 Web – www.naacp.org

Orchard Street Cultural Museum
24 South Abington Avenue
Baltimore 21229   (410) 669-3100

Cambridge

Stanley Institute and Christ Rock
Route No. 4, Box 1199
Cambridge 21613 – 1199   (410) 228-6657
E-Mail – zipcode@intercom.net
Type of Museum – Historic House
Director – Herschel Johnson   Founded - 1867

Columbia

African Art Museum of Maryland
5430 Vantage Point Road
P.O. Box 1105
Columbia 21044-0105 (410) 730-7106 Fax (410) 730-7105
Web –Africanartmuseum.org
E-Mail – Africanartmuseum@erols.com
Type of Museum – Art
Director – Doris Ligon Founded - 1980

Howard County Center of African - American Culture
5434 Vantage Point Rd.
Columbia 21644   (410) 715 – 1921

Hagerstown

Marquente Doleman House Museum
54019 Locust Street
Hagerstown 21740 (301) 739-8185
Director - Marquente Doleman Founded - 1975

LaPlata Afro-American Heritage Society Museum
7485 Crain Highway
LaPlata 20646
(301) 843-0371

Waldorf

Afro-American Heritage Museum
925 North High
Box 316
Waldorf 20601   (410) 843-0371

MASSACHUSETTS

Boston

National Center for Afro – American Artists
360 Huntington Avenue - Building 590
Northeastern University-Mickelson Hall
Boston 02115 (617) 437-3139 Founded - 1977

African Meeting House
8 Smith Court
Boston 02114 (617) 723-8863

Harriet Tubman Gallery
United South End Settlement
566 Columbus Avenue
Boston 02118 (617) 536-8610

Museum of Afro-American History
46 Joy Street
14 Beacon St. Suite 719 Administrative Office
Boston 02114 (617) 725-0022 Fax (617) 720-5225
Web – Aframmuseum.org E-Mail History@afroammuseum.org
Type of Museum – History Director- Beverly A. Morgan – Welch   Founded - 1967

Museum of Afro-American History
719 Tremont Street
Boston 02118-3417 (617) 445-7400

Museum of the National Center of Afro-American Artists
300 Walnut Avenue
Boston 02119 (617) 442-8614   Fax (617) 445 - 5525
E-Mail – Bgaither@mfa.org   Type of Museum - Art
Director - Edmund Barry Gaither   Founded - 1968

Nantucket

African Meeting House On Nantucket
Nantucket Historical Association
29 York Street
P.O. Box 2637
Nantucket 02584-2182   (508) 228-9833

Plymouth

Parting Ways: Museum of Afro-American Ethnic History, Inc.
130 Court Street
Plymouth 02360   (508) 746-6028 Founded - 1974

Springfield

African-American Museum and Cultural Center of Western Massachusetts
P.O. Box 4033
Springfield 01101 (413) 737-9290

Afro-American Cultural Center
30 Concord Terrace
Springfield 01109

MICHIGAN

Ann Arbor

African American Cultural and Historical Museum
1100 N. Main Street
Suite 201 –C
Ann Arbor 48104

Benton Harbor

African American Hall of Fame Museum
153 W. Main St.
Benton Harbor 49002-3607   (269) 926-7844

Detroit

Abibiman Treasurer of Black Arts Museum
18334 Livonor Avenue
Detroit 48226   (313) 861-1510
Co-Founders - Albert & Breanda Nuamah

Black Holocaust Museum
13335 Livernois Ave.
Detroit 48238 (313) 491-0777

Black Legends of Professional Basketball
8900 E. Jefferson Ste. 328
Detroit 48214   (313) 822-8208   Fax (313) 822-8227

Gospel Music Hall of Fame And Museum
18301 W. McNichols
Detroit 48219   (313) 592 – 0017   Fax (313) 592-8762

Graystone International Jazz Museum
3000 East Grand Boulevard
Detroit 48202   (313) 871-0234
Director - James Jenkins   Founded - May 1974

Motown Historical Museum
2648 West Grand Boulevard
Detroit 48208 (313) 875-2264 Fax (313) 875-2267
Web - Motownmuseum.org E-Mail motownmus@aol.com
Type of Museum - Music & History Director - Robin Terry   Founded - 1985

Charles H. Wright Museum of African-American History
315 East Warren Ave.
Detroit 48202 (313) 494 – 5800
Web – www.maah-detroit.org Founded - March 1965

28

The National Afro-American Sports Hall of Fame and Gallery
Wayne County Building, 4th Floor
600 Randolph
Detroit
(Mailing address:
P.O. Box 27615
149 California Street
Highland Park, MI 48203
(313) 272-0281   (313) 865-7906, or 571- 4444
Founder - Elmer Anderson   Founded - 1982

The National Museum of the Tuskegee Airman
6325 West Jefferson
Detroit 48209   (313) 843-8849

Your Heritage House
110 East Ferry Street
Detroit 48202   (313) 871-1667 Founded 1969

Flint

Greater Flint Afro-American Hall of Fame
36 Pingree
Flint 48503   (313) 743-8795
President - Norman Bryant   Founded - 1983

The Flint Museum of African-American History
3509 Burgess
Flint 48504   (313) 785-4553
Director - Kathryn Williams   Founded - 1984

Museum of Afrikan American History – Flint
2712 North Saginaw Street   Suite 13 – E
Flint 48505-4479 (810) 233 – 5606

Mississippi

Jackson

Medgar Evers Museum
2332 Margaret Walker Alexander Drive
Jackson 39204 (601) 981-2965 Tours (601) 977-7710

Smith Robertson Black Cultural Center
528 Bloom Street
Jackson 39202   (601) 960-1457   Fax (601) 960-2070
Web- City.Jackson.ms.us
Type of Museum - History
Director – Pamela D.C. Junior   Founded - August 1983

Lexington

Fannie Booker-Thomas Museum
Highway 12 West,TCHula Road
Route 2 - Box 314T   { By appointment }
Lexington 39095   (601) 834-2672
Director - Fannie Booker

Natchez

Natchez Museum of Afro-American History
301 Main Street
Natchez 39120 (601) 445-0728   Fax (601) 445-0728

Tougaloo

Tougaloo College Art Museum
Warren Hall
Tougaloo 39174 (601) 956-4941

Vicksburg

Vicksburg Afro-American Museum/Studio, Inc.
P.O. Box 122
Vicksburg 39181   (601) 638-9201 (601) 638-3890
Founded – 1989

Jacqueline House African American Museum
1325 Main Street
Vicksburg 39183-2647   (601) 636-0941   (601) 638-7304

Missouri

Ash Grove

Ozarks Afro-American Heritage Museum
107 West Main Street
P.O. Box 265
Ash Grove 65604   (417) 672-3104   (417) 751-9753

Kansas City

    Kansas City Jazz Museum & Negro League Baseball Museum
1616 East 18th Street
Kansas City 64108
(816) 871- 3016 Fax (816) 221-8424
Director - Lloyd Johnson

    Bruce R. Watkins Cultural Heritage Center
3700 Blues Parkway
Kansas City 64130 (816) 923-6226
Founded - 1988

    Black Archives of Mid-America
2023 Vine Street
Kansas City 64108 (816) 483-1300
Director - Horace Peterson III Founded - 1974

St. Louis

    Black World History Museum
2505 St. Louis Ave.
St. Louis 63106 (314) 241 – 7045

    Scott Joplin House
2658-60 Delmar Boulevard
St. Louis 63103 (314) 533-1003
Director - Annette Bridges Founded - 1990

    Vaughn Cultural Center
5205 North Grand
St. Louis 63102 (314) 535-9227
Director - Almetta Jordan Founded – 1977

NEBRASKA

Omaha

    Great Plains Black Museum
2213 Lake Street
Omaha 68110 (402) 345-2212
Director - Bertha Calloway Founded - February 1976

NEVADA

Las Vegas

    The Walker African American Museum & Research Center
705 W. Van Buren Ave.
Las Vegas 89106 (702) 647- 2242

NEW JERSEY

Jersey City

Afro-American Historical and Cultural Society of Jersey City
1841 Kennedy Boulevard
Jersey City 07305 (201) 547-5262 Fax (201) 547-5392
Director - Theodore Brunson Founded - 1977

Newark

The International Black History Museum and Cultural Center
P.O. Box 20208
Newark 07101 (201) 371-3040

Tenafly

SMA African Arts Museum
23 Bliss Avenue
Tenafly 07670 (201) 894- 8611 Fax (201) 541- 1280
Web – Smafathers.org E-Mail – Smausa@smafathers.org
Type of Museum - Art
Director – Robert J. Koenig Founded - 1965

Willingboro

Marabash Museum
P.O. Box 752
Willingboro 08046 (609) 877-3177
Director - Mark Henderson Founded – 1973

NEW YORK

Brooklyn

New Muse Community Museum of Brooklyn
1530 Bedford Avenue
Brooklyn 11216 (718) 774-2900
Director - Greer Smith Founded - 1975

Simmons Collection of African Arts Museum
1063 Fulton Street
Brooklyn 11238 (718) 230-0933
Director/Curator - Stanfield Simmons Founded - 1983

Society for Preservation of Weeksville & Bedford-Stuyvesant History
1698 Bergen Street
Brooklyn 11213 (718) 756 - 5250
Director - John Maynard Founded - 1968 Chartered – 1971

Buffalo

Afro-American Historical Society of the Niagara Frontier
P.O. Box 63
Buffalo 14207 (716) 886-1399 (716) 858-7194
Director - Dr. Monroe Fordham Founded - 1974

Langston Hughes Institutes, Inc.
Center for Cultural History & Arts Education
25 High Street
Buffalo 14203 (716) 881-3266 Fax (716) 881-2372
E-Mail – LHIBuffalo@adelphia.net
Type of Musueum – Art, Music, Cultural & Memorabilia

Museum of African and Afro-American Art and Antiquities
11 East Utica Street
Buffalo 14209 (716) 882-7676
Director - Glendora Johnson

Hempstead

African-American Museum of Nassau County
110 North Franklin Street
Hempstead 11550 (516) 572-0730 Fax (516) 572-0732
Type of Museum - History
Director – Willie Houston Founded - 1970

Jamaica

Storefront Museum/Paul Roberson Theatre
19545 Jamaica Avenue
Jamaica 11432-2639 (718) 523-5199
Executive Director - Tom Lloyd Founded - 1971

New York

Adam Clayton Powell, Jr. Museum
Abyssinian Baptist Church
130 Odell Clark Place
New York City 10030 (212) 862-7474 or 7475

African American Wax and History Museum
318 West 115th Street
New York 10026 (212) 678-7818 (212) 678-5009

Aunt Len's Doll and Toy Museum
Six Hamilton Terrace
New York City 10031 (212) 281-4143 or 926-4172
Director - Lenon H. Hoyte Founded - 1962

Black Fashion Museum, Harlem Institute of Fashion
155-57 West 126th Street
New York City 10027 (212) 666-1320
Director - Lois K. Alexander Founded - October 1979

Genesis II Museum of International Black Culture
Manhattan 10025 (212) 666-7222
Director - Andi Owens Founded - 1972 (museum opened 1990)

Grinnell Gallery
800 Riverside Drive
New York City 10032   (212) 927-7941
Co-Directors - Pat Davis & Dr. Ademola Olugebfola   Founded - 1977

Hatch-Billops Collection
491 Broadway - 7th Floor
New York, 10012   (212) 966-3231

Schomburg Center for Research in Black Culture
New York Public Library
515 Malcolm Blvd.
New York City 10037-1801   (212) 481 - 2263
Director - Howard Dodson   Founded - 1925

Studio Museum in Harlem
144 West 125th Street
New York City 10027   (212) 864-4500 Fax (212) 864-4800
Web - Studiomuseum.org Type of Museum – Art
Director – Dr. Lowery Stokes Sims Founded - 1968

319 Gallery
319 West 108th Street
New York City 10025
Director - Linda Bryant

Peeskill

Westchester African-American Historical Society
1126 Howard Street
Peeskill 10566   (914) 737-2606
Director - Kay Amory-Mosler   Founded June – 1985

Queens

Louis Armstrong's House and Archives
Queens College-SUNY
34 - 56 107th Street,
New York 11368
(718) 478- 8274 or 8297

The Underground Railroad
214-21 113th Avenue
New York 10026-3306

Rochester

Frederick Douglass Museum & Cultural Center
25 East Main Street Suite 500
Rochester 14614-1874   (716) 546-3960   Fax (716) 546-7218

Syracuse

Community Folk Art Gallery
2223 East Genesee Street
Syracuse 13210   (315) 424-8487
Director - Herbert Williams Founded - 1972

Valhalaha

Madame C.J. Walker Museum and Afro-American Cultural Foundation
c/o Westchester Community College
75 Grasslands Road
Valhalaha 10595   (914) 347-2211
Director - John Harmon

North Carolina

Ashville YMI Cultural Center
39 South Market Street
Asheville 28801 (828) 252-4614   Fax (828) 257-4539
Web – ymicc.org E-Mail – ymicc1@aol.com
Type of Museum - Cultural
Director – Rita Martin Founded – 1893

Charlotte

Afro-American Cultural Center
401 North Myers Street
Charlotte 28202 (704) 374-1565 Fax (704) 374-9273
Web – Aacc- Charcotte.org   E-Mail- Alccia@aacc-Chariotte.org
Type of Museum – Cultural   Director – Alecia Bracy Founded – 1974

Durham

Charlotte-Mecklenburg Afro-American Cultural Service Center
North Carolina Central University Museum of Art
1805 Fayetteville Street
Durham 27707   (919) 683-6211
Director - Norman Pendergraft   Founded -1971

Museum of African American Art
804 Old Fayetteville St.
Durham 27701 (919) 683- 1709

Greensboro

Mattye Reed African Heritage Center
2711 McConnell Road
Greensboro 27401   (919) 379-7874 Founded 1968

Salisbury

The Heritage Hall
Livingstone College
West Monroe Street
Salisbury 28144   (704) 638-5500

Eden

The Martin Luther King Museum of Black Culture
511 North Henry Street
Eden 27288

Sedalia

Charlotte Hawkins Brown Historical Foundation, Inc.
Drawer G
Sedalia 27342   (919) 449-6515

Ohio

Akron

Watkins Academy Museum of Cultural Arts
724 Mineola Avenue
Akron 44320   (216) 864-0673
Director - James Watkins   Founded – 1976

Cincinnati

Art Consortium African American Museum Union Terminal
Mailing Address 1515 Linn Street
1301 Western Ave.
Cincinnati 45214 (513) 381-0916 Fax (513) 381-0915
Web - In Progress   E-Mail - Toilynn@nattiarts.org
Type of Museum - Art & History   Director - Toilynn O'Neal   Founded - 1993

Cleveland

Afro-American Cultural Center
Black Studies Program Cleveland State University
2121 Euclid Avenue
Cleveland 44115   (216) 687-3655 Director - Professor Curtis Wilson

African-American Cultural and Historical Society Museum
1765 Crawford Road
Cleveland 44106   (216) 791-1700
Director - Booker T. Hall   Founded - 1953

Harriet Tubman Museum and Cultural Association
9250 Miles Park Avenue
Cleveland 44120-0178   (216) 663-1115   Fax (216) 341-1201
Director - Hanif Wahab   Founded - 1986

Dayton

Paul Laurence Dunbar House State Memorial
219 North Laurence Dunbar Street
Dayton 45407   (937) 224-7061   Director - Eva F. Peterson   Founded - 1938
Email – pldunbar1@aol.com   web- ohiohistory.org/places/dunbar/

Findlay

Black Studies & Library Association of Findlay and Hancock Counties
817 Harmon Street
Findlay 45840 (419) 423- 4954
President - Nina G. Parker   Founded - 1982

Wilberforce

National Afro-American Museum and Cultural Center
1350 Brush Row Road
Wilberforce 45384   (937) 376 – 4944   Fax – (937) 376-2007
Web - Places/afroam/index.html Type of Museum - History
Director – Vernon Courtney   Founded - 1978

Youngstown

>Afro-American Music Bicentennial Hall of Fame and Museum, Inc.
>P.O. Box 3901
>Youngstown 44505   (216) 746-7189
>Director - Frank E. Halfaore   Founded – 1969

OKLAHOMA

Oklahoma City

>Sanamu African Art Museum
>2100 Northeast 52nd Street
>Oklahoma City 73111   (405) 427-5461
>Director - Mary Ann Haliburton

>NTU Art Association-Kirkpatrick Center
>2100 North 52nd Street
>Oklahoma City 73111   (405) 424-7760
>Director - Hannah Atkins   Founded – 1979

PENNSYLVANIA

Philadelphia

>African-American Heritage, Inc.
>4610 Market
>Philadelphia 19139-3622 (215) 4716

>Afro-American Historical and Cultural Museum
>701 Arch Streets
>Philadelphia 19106   (215) 574-0380
>Director - Rowena Stewart   Founded – 1976

>Maria Anderson Historical Residence/Museum
>762 Marian Anderson Way
>Philadelphia 19146   (856) 966-1688   Fax (215) 732-1247
>blanche@marianaderson.org

>Mother Bethel A.M.E. Church
>419 Richard Allen Avenue
>Philadelphia 19147   (215) 925-0616
>Director - Ruby Boyd   Founded - 1787

>John W. Coltrane House and Society
>1511 North 33rd Street
>Philadelphia 19121-3513
>215-763-1118

Philadelphia Doll Museum
2253 North Broad Street
Philadelphia 19132   (215) 787-0220   Fax (215) 787-0226
Web - Philadollmuseum.com E-Mail – Dollmuse@aol.com
Type of Museum – History & Dolls Owner - Barbara Whiteman   Founded - 1988

Reading

Central Pennsylvania African American Museum
Old Bethel African Methodist Episcopal Church
119 N. Tenth St.
Reading 19601 (610) 371- 8713 Fax (610) 371- 8739

York

Crispus Attucks Community Center
605 South Duke Street
York 17403 (717) 848-3610

RHODE ISLAND

Providence

Rhode Island Black Heritage Society
The Arcade 65 Weybosset
Providence 02903   (401) 751-3490   Fax (401) 751-0040
Web – Providencericom/ri-blackheritage/
E-Mail – Blkheritage@netzero.net Type of Museum - History
Director – Joaquina Bela Teixeira   Founded – 1974

SOUTH CAROLINA

Charleston

Avery Institute of African American History and Culture
125 Bull Street
Charleston 29403 (843) 953-7609 Fax (843) 953-7607
Web – cof c.edu/avery   E-Mail – chandlerk.@cofc.edu
Type of Museum – History & Library
Director – Karen Chandler Founded – in 1985- Museum open in 1990

Columbia

Museum of African American Culture Manns - Simons Cottage
1601 Richland Street
Columbia 29201   (803) 252-1770 Fax (803) 929-7695
Web – historiccolumbia. Org   email – aposner@historiccolumbia.org
Type of Museum – Historic H
Director – Roger Poston   Founded – 1978

Darlington

Darlington Cultural Realism Charm
Darlington County County Museum Of Ethnic History
114 Coker Street
Darlington 29532   (803) 393-7052   Founded –1973

Pendleton

>Pendleton Foundation for Black History and Culture
>116 West Queen Street
>P.O. Box 122
>Pendleton 29670   (803) 646-3792
>Director – Annie Ruth Morse   Founded- 1976

St. Helena Island

>Penn Center – Foremore Plantation
>Martin Luther King Dr.
>St. Helena Island 29920- 0126   (843) 838 -2432
>Director- Emory Campbell   Founded – 1862

Sullivans Island

>Miriam B. Wilson Foundation/ Old Slave Mart
>Museum and Library
>P. O. Box 446
>Sullivan Island 29482   (803) 883-3797
>Founded 1962

TENNESSEE

Chattanooga

>Chattanooga African-American Museum and Research Center
>730 East Martin Luther King Boulevard
>Chattanooga 37401   (423) 267-1076   Fax (423) 267-10756
>E-Mail- caammuseumehotmail.com   Web-caamhistory
>Type of Museum – History & Cultural
>Director - Vilma Scruggs Fields   Founded – 1983

>Mary Walker Historical and Educational Foundation
>3031 Wilcox Blvd.
>Chattanooga 37411   (615) 622-3217
>Founded 1974

Henning

>Alex Haley State Historic Site and Museum
>200 South Church Street
>P.O. Box 500
>Henning 38041 (901) 738-2240
>Founded 1986 (as a museum)

Knoxville

>Beck Cultural Exchange Center
>1927 Dandridge Avenue
>Knoxville 37915-1909   (865) 524-8461   Fax (865) 524-8462
>Web – Kornet.org/beckcec email- Beckcec@korrnet.org
>Type of Museum – History
>Director - Kenneth Booker Founded - 1975

Memphis

National Civil Rights Museum/ Lorraine Civil Rights Museum
Lorraine Motel
450 Mulberry Street
Memphis 38103   (901) 521-9699
www.civilrightsmuseum.org Director - Juanita Moore   Founded - 1990

Nashville

Fisk University Museum of Art
D.B. Todd Boulevard and Jackson Street North
Nashville 37203   (615) 329-8543 or 8544
Curator - Pearl Creswell   Founded - 1949
Mailing address:
P.O. Box 2
Nashville 37203

TEXAS

Austin

Black Texans' Hall of Fame
920 East 11th Street
P.O. Box 141038
Austin 78753 (512) 837-1405

George Washington Carver Museum/Public Library
1165 Angelina Street
Austin 78702 (512) 472 - 4809
Director - Angela S. Medearis - Converted to museum in 1979

Dallas

African-American Cultural Heritage Center
Nolan Estes Educational Plaza
3434 S.R.L. Thornton Freeway
Dallas 75224   (214) 375-7530 Director - Laura J. Lacy   Founded - 1978

James Kemp Gallery
Dallas Convention Center
650 Griffin Street
Dallas 75202 (214) 743-2440 Fax (214) 743-2451
Type of Museum – Art - Director - Curtis King Founded – 1980

Museum of African-American Life & Culture
P.O. Box 41511
Dallas 75241
214-565-9026 or 372-8738 - Director:Dr.Harry Robinson, Jr
Founded 1974(moved from Bishop College in 1979)

South Dallas Cultural Center
1919 2nd Avenue
Dallas 75210 (214) 426-1806

Fort Worth

    Tarrant County Black Historical and
Genealogical Society, Inc.
1020 East Humboldt Street/
1150 East Rosedale Street
Fort Worth 76104
817-332-6049 Director: Lendra Rolla - Founded 1977

Houston

    African-American Heritage Museum
2101 Crawford - Suite 111A
Houston 77002
713-759-0044 Director: Dr. Robert Galloway - Founded 1988

    Buffalo Soldiers National Museum
1834 Southmore
Houston 77004 (713) 942-8920 Fax (713) 942-8912
E-mail –matthews@buffalosoldiermuseum.com

    Midtown Art Center/Kuumba House
3414 LaBranch
Houston 77004
713-524-1079

    Black Heritage Gallery
5408 Almeda Road - Suite 200
Houston 77004
713-529-7900 Director: Robbie E. Lee

    Texas Southern University
University Library Special Collections
3201 Wheeler Avenue
Houston 77004 (713) 313-4416

San Antonio

    Carver Community Cultural Center
226 North Hackberry
San Antonio 78202 (210) 207-7211 Fax – (210) 207- 4412
Web- The carver.org   E-Mail – chrisn@the craver.org
Type of Museum – Art, Music, Cultural & Film/Audio Visual
Director – William Lewis III   Founded – 1905

VIRGINIA

Alexandria

    Alexandria Black History Resource Center
638 N. Alfred Street
Alexandria 22314 (703) 838-4356 Fax (703) 706-3999
Web – Alexblackhistory.org Constructed - 1940, reopened - June 25,1983
E-Mail – Black.history@ci.alexblackhistory.org
Type of Museum – History - Director – Louis C. Hicks

Hampton
>Hampton University Museum
>Hampton 23668
>804-722-5308 Director: Jeanne Zeidler - Founded 1868

Richmond
>Black History Museum and Cultural Center, Inc.
>00 Clay
>Richmond 23219 (804) 780-9093 Fax (804) 780-9107
>Founded 1981 (officially conveyed Jan. 25, 1988)

>Maggie L. Walker National Historic Site
>600 N. Second Street
>Richmond 23219 (804) 771- 2017 - Founded - 197

Roanoke
>Harrison Museum of African American Culture
>523 Harrison Avenue N.W.
>P.O. Box 194
>Roanoke 24016 (703) 345-4818 - Director - Melody Stovall

Suffolk
>Phoenix Bank of Nansemond [Pending opening]
>300 East Washington Street
>Suffolk 23434-4516

WASHINGTON

Seattle
>Black Heritage Society of
>Washington State, Inc.
>P.O. Box 22565
>Seattle 98122 (206) 325-8205 (206) 723-0335
>Director - Joseph Warner Founded - 1977

Tacoma
>African American Museum
>925 Court C
>Tacoma 98402 (253)274-1278

WISCONSIN

Milwaukee
>Wisconsin Black Historical Society/Museum
>P.O. Box 11887
>Milwaukee 53211 (414) 372-7677
>Director - Clay Benson Founded – 1988

America's Black Holocaust Museum (ABHM)
2233 North 4th Street
Milwaukee 53212   (414) 264-2500   Fax (414) 264 - 0112
Web – Blackholocaustmuseum.org E-Mail – Abhmwi@aol.com
Type of Museum – History
Director - James Cameron   Founded - 1988

AFRICAN-AMERICAN MUSEUMS IN CANADA

ONTARIO

Amherstrurg

North American Black Historical Museum and Cultural Centre
277 King Street
Amherstrurg, Ontario N9V2C7   (519) 736-5433   (519) 736 – 5434
1-(800) 713-6336   Fax (519) 736-5433   Call First
Web –Blackhistoricalmuseum.com   E-Mail – nabhm@emporium.on.ca
Type of Museum - History
Director – Elise Harding – Davis   Founded - October 1975

North Buxton

Buxton National Historic Site & Museum
P.O. Box 3A, Comp1
21975 A.D. Shadd Road
North Buxton, Ontario N0P IY0
(519) 352-4799   Fax (519) 352-8561
Web – buxtonmuseum.com   E-Mail – buxton@ciaccess.com
Type of Museum – History Director – Shannon Prince   Founded - 1967

Puce

John Freeman Walls Historic Site
932 Concession 6 RR3
Essex, Ontario N8X 1M4   www.undergroundrailroadmuseum.com
(519) 258-6253   Fax (519) 727-4911

Toronto

Akwaa-Harrison Gallery
183 Queen Street East
Toronto, Ontario M5A 1S2 (0) Director - Richard Harrison   Founded - 1988
(416) 291-5496   (416) 947-1379

The Ontario Black History Society
Ontario Heritage Centre
10 Adelaide Street East - Suite 202
Toronto, Ontario M5C 1J3
(416) 867-9420
Director - Glace W. Lawrence   Founded - 1978

Windsor

Hiram Walker Historical Museum
254 Pitt Street West
Windsor, Ontario N9AA 5L5
(519) 253-1812   Founded - 1958

Nova Scotia

Dartmouth

Black Cultural Center for Nova Scotia
P.O. Box 2128
East Dartmouth, Nova Scotia B2W 3Y2
(902) 434-6223
Director - Birdglal Pachai   Founded – 1977

Dresden

Uncle Tom's Cabin Historic Site #40
29251 Uncle Tom's Road
Dresden, Ontario N0P 1M0
519) 683-2978   Fax (519) 683-1256
web – uncletomscabin.org   email – info@uncletomscabin.org
Type of Museum – History
Director – Steven Cook   Founded – 1984

CHAPTER 3

"The education and training of our children must not be limited to the Three R's, (reading, writing and arithmetic) only. It should instead include the history of the Black Nation, the knowledge of civilizations of man and the universe, and all sciences. It is necessary that the young people of our Nation learn all they can. Learning is a great virtue, and I would like to see all the children of my followers became the possessors of it. It will make us an even greater people tomorrow."

Elijah Muhammad

ALABAMA

Florence

> W.C. Handy Museum
> 620 W. College Street
> Florence, Al 35630
> (205) 760-6434

William Christopher Handy, popularly acclaimed "Father of the Blues," was born in a log cabin in Florence, Alabama on November 16, 1873. He died in New York City on March 29, 1958. Handy who gained fame and fortune, as the composer of the St. Louis Blues, Memphis Blues, and Beale Street Blues, was the first musician to write and preserve the blues songs for America's musical heritage. By so doing, he did more to bring blues songs into the mainstream of contemporary music than any other composer. Displayed are Handy's personal effects, instruments, citations from famous persons, and a wealth of other memorabilia.

He saved money for a guitar, only to be told by his father, an A.M.E. Methodist Minister, that he must trade it for something useful – a dictionary. The trade was made, but he soon saved enough money for a cornet. Then, at every opportunity, he studied and played music. To support him, he tried foundry work; school teaching and finally he formed his own band. Almost penniless, the band arrived at the Chicago World's Fair to find it had been postponed a year.

Not to be outdone, he taught at Huntsville A&M. By 1902, Handy was in Memphis where a mayoral campaign song for Mr. Crump became "The Memphis Blues." Music lovers universally know his 1914 "St. Louis Blues."

The road was not easy. In his autobiography, Handy said, "I have always imagined that hardship went into the making of the St. Louis Blues. When, much later, that whole song reflects a life filled with hard times as well as good times … Every time my soul, I think, occupied … a good bed in Florence, I had a stone for a pillow. I would hear an inner voice saying, 'your father was right, your proper place is studying for the ministry!' I was a prodigal son and there were few husks to eat, but when I would decide to arise and go to my softer bed in Florence, another voice would say, 'No! You will fight it out in spite of your adversities.'"

That determination, combined with incredible talent and memory, produced more than 100 songs, a music publishing company, and inspiration for thousands of musicians, a dozen books and worldwide admiration.

When Handy, nearly blind, died in March 28, 1958, the world mourned the loss of a composer, musician, publisher and friend. W. C. Handy said" … If my serenade of song and story should serve as a pillow for some composer's head, yet perhaps unborn, I will not have labored in vain. If, as my teacher predicted, music brought me to the gutter, I confess it was there I got a glimpse of heaven, for music can lift one to the state."

Normal

> State Black Archives Research Center and Museum
> P.O. Box 595
> Normal, Alabama 35762
> (256) 372-5846

"Providing a dialogue between the present and the past" - Sankofa (Go back to fetch it)

The primary purpose of the State Black Archives Research Center and Museum is to create a repository of resource materials on African American history and culture. Its mission is three fold:

- As an archive, to obtain, preserve and hold materials on African-American history and culture made available to scholars and others who seek materials for educational and cultural purposes.
- As a research center, to make such material on African Americans and culture available to scholars and others who seek materials for educational and cultural purposes.
- As a museum, to display materials on African-Americans in such a manner as to enhance the general public awareness about African-American history and culture.

The repository is housed in the James H. Wilson Building, which is a National Register for Historic structure on the campus of Alabama A & M University and was restored for the used of the State Black Archives Research Center & Museum. A bill, establishing the State Black Archives Research Center & Museum was passed by the State legislature in 1987 with the repository opening in 1990.

Several Display Exhibits

"Buffalo Soldier and the Ignoble Mission"
"Kwanzaa"
"Making Their Mark"
"The African American Architects and Architecture"
"Black Women Against the Odds"
"Mardi Gras Indian"
"A Rich Heritage and a Continuing Legacy"

Wetumka

The Elmore County Black History Museum
1004 Lancaster Street
Wetumpka, Al 36092
(334) 567-5330

In 1986, members of the black community of Elmore County with help from the City of Wetumpka and the Park Board took a giant step in turning the Old Elmore County Training School into a museum of Black History. Although the Elmore Training School was built in 1984 for Black students in the days of segregation – days when Black students went to Black schools and white students went to White school – the Training School was the only high school for students in the area. In 1962, the county wanted to abandon the Elmore County Training school, and raze the building for a public park for Negroes.

The potential for preservation of the Elmore County Training School building captured the attention and imagination of former Wetumpka mayor Jeannette Barrett as she pondered a use for the historic structure. The board of Education had deeded the structure and property to the city. "That school was built in 1924. It is a black landmark and is eligible for the National Register of Historic Places" Barrett said. "I felt that that it could be an economic asset to our community. It was too good to tear down," she said.

The City of Wetumpka received a $15,000.00 grant from the state to renovate the training school building on Lancaster Street behind the cemetery on Wetumpka west side. The building was constructed in 1924. The money was used to install ceiling fans, repair floors, and brick windows to shield artifacts from light and to preserve them.

The museum's permanent collection focuses on the histories of Elmore County Black families, Black schools and Black churches. On display in the museum is an Elmore County map with locations of black churches. Standing in a window box is a mirror that once belonged to the famous boxer from Alabama, Joe Louis. A retired Air Force Lieutenant Colonel who lives in Ozark County Black families, churches, schools and civic organizations, donated the mirror. The collection is designed to stimulate interest of Black American family and community history in Elmore County, and to raise the consciousness of the public in appreciation and research in the history of a people whose heritage and history has generally been unrecognized.

ARKANSAS

Pine Bluff

Leedell Moorehead – Graham Fine Arts Gallery
University of Arkansas at Pine Bluff
1200 North University Ave.
Pine Bluff, Arkansas 71601
(870) 575-8236

Persistence of the Spirit – The Black Experience in Arkansas

Persistence of the Spirit presents a new look at over 300 years of the Black presence and participation in Arkansas history.

The project's premise, when it began in March 1984, was that most people knew very little about Black history in this state. While there was an abundance of small articles on many aspects of that experience, in general, more detailed or comprehensive materials were hard to find. No books that covered this rich history fairly – or even adequately, could be found. For teachers, students, and general adult readers, it was difficult to fit the Black experience of the past into the larger scope of Arkansas or American history.

So, project researchers undertook to collect, organize and review what had already been written and to reinterpret that body of work while adding new resources written and visual.

The themes analyzed include slavery; the impact of Black labor on the development of the state; and the skill and creativity of Black Arkansans in agriculture, politics, education, labor, business and religion. Running throughout are the connecting threads: the strength and determination of the family in attaining their goals, the sacrifices and enduring successes, and the persistent cycle tension between the hopes of Black people and the working of the larger society.

The result is a permanent exhibit of 27 panels (measuring 8`x108`) that is now open to the public in the West Gallery of the Isaac Hathaway Fine Arts Center at the University of Arkansas at Pine Bluff. It is a blend of historical scholarship and visual documentation that serves as a beginning for understanding the varied perspectives and enduring traditions of Black Arkansans. For 300 years, they have dealt with their world and helped shape it. Against heavy odds, they have "Persisted".

CALIFORNIA

Los Angeles

California Afro-American Museum
600 State Drive Exposition Park
Los Angeles, California 90037
(213) 744-7432

"Keeper of the Flame"

The California Afro-American Museum has as its primary goal the collection and preservation of artifacts documenting the Afro-American experience in this country. The museum was established by the State of California in 1977. CAAM began operation in 1981 as one of the first state mandated museums of its kind in the nation.

On March 22, 2003, the California African-American Museum opened after a 3 million dollar renovation. Improvements made to the museum included new heating and air-conditioning systems, new roof, hardwood floors in all three of the galleries, a state – of – the – art security system, improved signage on the building and improved storage areas, as well as climate control for preserving the art in the collection. In addition the museum is now equipped with a state – of –the – art sound system and shades for the Sculpture Court to protect the art and artifacts exhibited in that space. These changes to the building allow for programs that are more accessible and inclusive, and ultimately have a greater impact on the community.

Built through state funding, corporate and community donations, CAAM is a focal point for cultural activity in the state.

Programs

Collections	Workshops
Exhibitions	Special Performances
Films	School Visits
Lectures	Publications Research
Museum Registry	Outreach

Los Angeles

Museum of African-American Art
4005 Crenshaw Boulevard – Third Floor
Los Angeles, California 90028-2534
(213) 294-7071

The Museum of African-American Art is the first of its kind in the Western United States. Noted artist and art historian Dr. Samella Lewis and a group of academic, artistic, business and community leaders organized the museum. Their fundamental goal was to support public awareness and artistic expression of African-American Art.

The museum library and archives are open to the public and are a significant asset to art scholars. The museum is a significant cultural force in Los Angeles, California, and the nation. Its unique location, within the May Company Department store, invites easy access and emphasizes the fact that art can and should be a part of our daily life.

The permanent collection of the Museum of African Art reflects one of the institution's fundamental goals: conserving the art of Africa and African – descendents. The collection includes paintings, sculptures, masks, batiks, carving and ceremonial objects from Africa, the Caribbean, the South Pacific, South America and the United States. The museum is the repository for the Palmer Hayden collection and archives, which together give the public an insight into the life and work of one of the leading artists of the Harlem Renaissance.

Los Angeles

African-American Firefighter Museum
1401 Central Ave.
Los Angeles, California 90021
(213) 744-1730

The African-American Firefighters Museum is a non- profit organization dedicated to collecting, conserving and sharing the heritage of African-American firefighters.

The museum is housed in Fire Station # 30, which was one of two segregated fire stations in Los Angeles between 1924 and 1955. This beautifully restored faculty has been designated as Los Angeles Historic – Cultural Monument #289, and is a recipient of the Los Angeles Conservancy's 1999 Preservation Award. Fire Station #30 was established in 1913 to serve the Central Avenue community.

The one hundred – year history of African-America firefighters in Los Angeles' fire service provides a glimpse of life from a unique perspective. Not only does the museum exhibit uniforms, badges, photograph, and other firefighting paraphernalia, we also engage our visitors in an examination of human relations through the stories of the "Old Stentorian." The experiences of desegregation offer an opportunity to explore and learn from the actions that allowed the African-American firefighter to excel despite adversity.

Oakland

Northern California Center
For Afro-American History & Life
5606 San Pablo Avenue
Oakland, California 94608
(415) 658-3158

The Northern California Center for Afro-American History and Life is a non-profit organization whose primary activities are aimed at collecting, preserving, interpreting and disseminating materials documenting the Afro-American experience and culture in California the West, and the United States. Founded in 1965, as the East Bay Negro Historical Society, the Center is directed by a noted historian and educator who are advised by a committee of Trustees from the northern section of the state. While the focus is Northern California and the state, the collections are international in scope.

The Center is a unique resource for the study of Afro-American history and culture. Students, researches, and educators will find the Center to be a rich repository of primary source and rare or unusual secondary and visual material.

Files on individual Black Californians, records of the organizations, and institutions of the Black community make up a large part of the Center's holdings. Beginning with the earliest explorers and settlers, Black Americans have been active players in the history if California. Among the first Black Americans in California were Spanish-speaking members of Spanish garrisons and exploring parties, gold-seeking Forty-Niners, members of the clergy, slaves, and a variety of enterprising individuals with a vision of opportunity.

As participants in the broad sweep of American and Western history, they sought new trails, built communities, moved from rural to urban occupations. At the same time, they were victims of discrimination which forced them to create their own institutions, and to nurture their own community resources to care for many different needs while developing distinctive Afro- American interpretations of the Western experience.

From the Gold Rush to the World War II defense industry boom, the lure of California has appealed in special ways to Black Americans, promising not only economic betterment and a congenial physical setting, but, also relief from the worst forms of racial discrimination. Although Afro-Americans have had to struggle continuously for such basic citizenship rights as access to public schools, the right to use the court system, and the right to live where they choose, the evolving institutions of California's young society were more readily influenced than those of more established Eastern states.

The present collection forms a nucleus for a steadily growing body of documentation. The Center is presently housed on the first floor of the Golden Gate Library at 56th street and San Pablo Avenue, in Oakland, California.

San Francisco

>San Francisco African-American
>Historical and Cultural Society
>Fort Mason Center
>Laguna & Marina Blvd.
>Building C Room 165
>San Francisco, California 94123
>(415) 441-0640

The San Francisco African-American Historical Society is one of the earliest continuous institutions of its kind in the West. Founded in 1955, the Society is a non-profit membership institution governed by a Board of Directors.

The Society's purpose is to preserve the history and promote the culture of the African-American people so that knowledge of their contributions may serve as an inspiration to all generations in the San Francisco Bay Area,

The Society's facility includes:

>Museum, Research Library, Gift Shop, Art Gallery
>Howard Thurman Listening Room

The Society collects artifacts and archival materials, which are preserved and displayed in the museum. The exhibitions that are shown in the gallery are works of new and master artists of African-American descent on the local, national and international level. The library has a large and growing collection of books, periodicals, and cataloged files that are available for reading and research on the premises.

COLORADO

Denver

>Black American West Museum
>608 26th Street
>Denver, Colorado 80205
>(303) 295-1026

We Tell it Like it Was

Did you know: Nearly a third of the cowboys in the "Wild West" were Black? Black families came west in covered wagons; they established self – sufficient all Black-towns, they filled every job from barber to teacher, doctor to state legislator.

They owned much of the West's most valuable real estate and many of its prominent businesses. They were some of the West's earliest millionaires. Blacks played a major role in settling and shaping the American West. Yet their story goes untold. No collection has brought together the artifacts and documents that tell the story.

Until Now!

The Black American West Museum and Heritage Center is the most comprehensive source of historic material on Blacks in the West. Personal artifacts, memorabilia, newspaper, legal documents, letters, photographs and oral histories make up its collection of 35,000 items. From the early fur trade until today, our exhibits document the Black contribution to Western life.

How the Museum Started

The Museum started as a personal hobby of Paul C. Stewart. As a child playing cowboys and Indians, Paul had to play an Indian because there was "no such thing as a Black cowboy". When as an adult, Paul met a Black cowboy - a man who had ridden cattle drives at the turn of the century – he vowed then and there to unearth all he material he could on other Black pioneers.

Paul C. Stewart settled in Denver, running a barbershop and raising a family. At the age of 40 Stewart began a new career as a Western historian. He closed his barbershop in 1975 and, with the help of some government and private funds; he founded the Black American West Museum and Heritage Center. Paul likes to take the part of a cowboy, from the brim of his cowboy hat to his black leather vest to the tips of his boots. He is writing a six volume series of books on Blacks in the West. His museum is packed with photographs. Paul thinks that this museum makes people feel differently and will change the way they think. "Paul Stewart is going to keep on working to get that message across". The story is still growing. The museum is still gathering memories, still adding to its collection.

- Dr. Justina Ford was Denver's first black woman doctor.

- Louis Price, a Black Millionaire in Denver at the turn of the 20th Century had four white servants and a White coachman.
- First gold discoveries in Idaho Springs, Colorado were made by Henry Parker, a Black mine owner.
- Many Blacks learned barbering during slavery. After the Civil War they opened their own barbershops. As a result, at the end of the 1800s, 90% of all barbers in the U.S. were Black.

What was the reason Blacks came West? Blacks came West for the same reason White came for: the gold and to strike it rich. In 1860, there were 46 Blacks in Colorado; by 1910 there were 11,453. Stewart has a seemingly endless supply of stories about the photos and items displayed.

Over the next 30 years, his search took him to every corner of the West and with each new contact, the story grew – the contribution of blacks was found to be larger.

CONNECTICUT

New Haven

Connecticut Afro-American Historical Society, Inc.
444 Orchard Street
New Haven, Connecticut 06511
(203) 776-4907

Founded in New Haven, Connecticut in 1971 this African-American Historical Society is dedicated to collecting and preserving historical biographies and events depicting the meaningful role African-Americans have had in building Connecticut and the United States.

A research center and museum, serving as the Society's headquarters, is currently located at 444 Orchard Street in New Haven. Here visitors may see periodicals, exhibits, and papers documenting numerous accomplishments made by African-American men and women down through the centuries.

Memorabilia commemorates the achievements of African-American educational, civic and cultural leaders, athletes, and military personnel and recognizes the churches and other organizations that help guide these men and women in their pursuits. In building this valuable resource library, the

Society collects biographies, directories, newspapers, handbills, programs, letters, diaries, rosters, photographs, relics and objects relating to past events and activities.

The Connecticut Afro-American Historical Society, Inc. believes the future for knowing and understanding its past rich heritage can fortify its race.

"To be ignorant of what occurred before you is to remain always a child. For what is the worth of human life, unless it is woven into the life of our ancestors by the record of history."
Cicero

DISTRICT OF COLUMBIA

Washington D.C.
Anacostia Museum
Smithsonian Institution
1001 Fort Place S.E.
Washington, D.C. 20020
(202) 287-3369

The Anacostia Museum opened at 2405 Martin Luther King Jr. Avenue, S.E., on September 15, 1967, as a branch of the Smithsonian Institution. Located in the historic community of Anacostia, the museum presents a wide range of changing exhibitions and programs on the history and culture of Afro – Americans.

The concept of a neighborhood museum was first set forth in the mid-1960s in a speech by then Smithsonian Secretary S. Dillon Ripley. Newspaper accounts of Ripley's speech resulted in inquiries from the Greater Anacostia.

Anacostia was selected as the location for the museum, and community groups helped to ready the building. Neighborhood residents, on the basis of suggestions from the Smithsonian, selected the objects on display for the opening. Included were a full-scale mock-up of a Mercury space capsule equipped with gadgets to simulate an actual flight; a "bone room" displaying skeletons that could be assembled and taken apart; a closed-circuit TV camera and monitor for children to view themselves and their friends; a small zoo, and an 1890 country store and post office.

In May 1987, the Anacostia Museum moved to 1901 Fort Place S.E., a building located in Fort Stanton Park, the site of a Civil War fort erected to protect the Navy Yard. The area is under the jurisdiction of the National Park Service. This facility also houses the museum's research and education departments, as well as the exhibits, design and production branches.

The museum serves the Washington, D.C., metropolitan area and a national audience. Several of its exhibitions are shown across the country under the auspices of the Smithsonian Institution Traveling Exhibition Service.

In its 20 years history, the museum has displayed a variety of exhibitions. The Barnett-Aden collection, the holdings of the first black-owned gallery in Washington, D.C., was shown at the museum. The history and culture of Black people have been the subjects of such exhibits as "Black Women: Achievements against the Odds" and "Out of Africa: From West African Kingdoms to Colonization." An exhibition on the Harlem Renaissance told the story of the period in the 1920's when black artists, writers and musicians demonstrated racial pride through their work.

The Anacostia story couldn't be told without telling the history of Anacostia from the beginning. As the local history unfolds, you find the village of the Nacotchtank Indians – from a rural setting, to a village and hamlet, to a small-town suburban area, and to an urban milieu with a variety of life-styles. In Anacostia's past there have been slaveholders with large plantations sharecroppers, blue-collar workers and craftsmen, professional and business people, religious leaders and politicians, young people and elders.

Washington, D.C.
>Bethune Museum and Archives, Inc.
>1318 Vermont Avenue, N.W.
>Washington, D.C. 20005
>(202) 332-1233 (202) 332-9201

Mary McLeod Bethune, a distinguished educator, political activist, and advisor to four Presidents of the United States, devoted her life to obtaining equal opportunity for African-American and for women in this country. Founder of Bethune-Cookman College and the National Council of Negro Women (NCNW), Bethune worked tirelessly to influence legislation affecting African American women and developed programs that sought to alleviate economic and social injustice. During Bethune's lifetime (1875-1955), she was one of the most influential and prominent African American women and was a political and educational leader in the United States.

The Bethune Museum and Archives National Historic Site originally opened in November 1979 and was granted National Historic Site status through an act of Congress in April 1982. Since 1983, the Bethune Museum and Archives has been a fully independent, non-profit organization that preserves the historic and contemporary contributions made by African-American women and enrich the lives of America's children through educational materials, programs and other services.

The Archival and photographic holdings of the Bethune Museum – Archives National Historic Site comprise the largest body of records relating to the history of African American women in a public repository. As such, these materials are an invaluable resource for historians, sociologists, journalists and others interested in obtaining information concerning the participation of African American women in the major social and political movements and events that have defined American History. This is the only institution of its kind.

Washington, D.C.
>The Black Fashion Museum
>2007 Vermont Ave. N.W.
>Washington, D.C.2001
>(202) 667-0744

The Black Fashion Museum (BFM) was founded in 1979 by Lois K. Alexander – Lane to celebrate centuries of contributions to fashion and design by Black women and men. Its mission also was to identify, acknowledge and spotlight the achievements and contributions of Black people to the fashion industry, past, present and future.

Throughout the United States, distinctive colors, shapes, styles and patterns have originated in the Black community, and then become mainstream fashion. Black designers and craftspeople have produced some of the finest garments and accessories in the world.

While doing research for her master's thesis "The Role of the Negro in Retailing in New York City from 1863 to the Present" (1963), Mrs. Alexander – Lane found little information on the contribution of Black designers. As a result of her research, she decided to dispel the myth that Black people are newly found talent in the creative fields of fashion, and to acquaint the Black community with yet another facet of its heritage. Black Fashion Museum (BFM) collects and displays garments and memorabililia that illustrate an important part of fashion history. From slave dresses to clothing by distinguished Black people of the past and present, the museum ensures that Black fashion is preserved and celebrated.

Washington, D.C.
> The Evans -Tibbs Collection
> 1910 Vermont Avenue, N. W.
> Washington, D.C. 20001
> (202) 234-8164

Thurlow Tibbs' major goal of his life is to rescue 19th and 20th century Black American artists from oblivion and integrate them into the mainstream of American Art History. He devotes a substantial part of his life and financial resources to collecting their works and searching out biographical material on them.

Tibbs has taken a townhouse at 1910 Vermont Avenue, N.W., Washington, D.C. that was his grandmother's property and the home he grew up in and turned it into the Evans – Tibbs Collection. This new identity has been turned into a commercial gallery and a germ of a museum on the second floor.

Another one of Tibbs' project is a bibliographic database consisting of Afro – American artists. He states that his library of close to 6,000 items is one of the best in the country – better for example than Howard University's library content in the same area.

Tibbs started his gallery in a spontaneous but informed way by lending space to two of his friends who were artists that needed to exhibit. As time went on, Tibbs expanded his collection and later incorporated the gallery in 1980, with old family friends on the board of directors.

In the next five years, Tibbs plans to catalog the entire collection. A question is posed, "Can Thurlow Tibbs Jr. move Washington to allow his project to develop to its fullest"? Tibbs himself is cautious about the future, but in spite of occasional frustrations, he finds the present just fine. "You cannot get in this unless you love it."

Washington, D.C.
> Fredrick Douglas National Historical Site
> 1411 W. S.E.
> Washington, D. C. 20020
> (202) 426-5960

The activities of the Fredrick Douglas Site start at the visitor center. You will find exhibits and a film that tell you about Douglas, plus publications and items pertaining to Douglas' African-American culture.

Fredrick Douglas was born in Talbot County Maryland 1818. The exact date is unknown. His mother was a slave and his father was White. Fredrick Douglas spent his early years in a home broken beyond most people's comprehension. His mother, a slave, was forced to leave him as an infant. At age 8 he was sent to Baltimore as a house servant. He became fascinated by the mystery of reading and decided that education was the pathway from slavery to freedom. Because it was illegal to educate slaves, Fredrick learned how to read and write by trading bread for reading lessons and tracing over words in discarded spelling books until his handwriting was smooth and graceful. Douglas lifetime triumphs were many: abolitionist, women's rights activist, author, and owner – editor of antislavery newspaper, fluent speaker of many languages, and minister to Haiti and most respected African American orator of the 19th century.

Douglas moved into this 1850's brick house that he named Cedar Hill. For 40 years he had battled for human rights, and Cedar Hill provided a welcome respite. In 1962 the care of Cedar Hill was entrusted to the National Park Service. Fredrick Douglass was deemed the "Sage of Anacostia," an accolade that celebrated the intellectual spirit within him that never grew old. "To those who have battled for liberty, and citizenship, I can say I, too, have battled".

Washington, D.C.
>Moorland – Spingarn Research Center
>Howard University
>Washington, D. C. 20059
>(202) 636-7115

Moorland – Spingarn Research Center is recognized as one of the world's largest and most comprehensive repositories for collections documenting the history and culture of people of African descent in the Americas, Africa and Europe. The Research Center is one of Howard University's major research facilities. Although the resources of the research center have been developed primarily for the use of Howard University faculty and students, all visitors are welcome. The reading room and other areas are designed for serious research. Since facilities for readers are limited, and because many of the materials are unique and cannot be replaced, conservation policies have been developed to retard deterioration of materials and preserve the integrity of the collection for future researchers.

The main divisions of the Research Center are the Library Division and the Manuscript Division. Major collections and units include the Jessie E. Moorland Collection, the Arthur B. Spingarn Collection, the Glenn Carrington Collection, the Ralph J. Bunche Oral History Collection, the Howard University Archives, the Black Press Archives, and the Howard University Museum. All collections of the Research Center are maintained as research collections and all materials must be used on the premises.

The holdings include more than one hundred thousand books, pamphlets, and periodicals; more than four hundred manuscript and archival collections; and thousands of microforms, sheet music, tapes, transcripts, photographs, records, and artifacts.

Washington, D.C.
>National Museum of African Art
>Smithsonian Institution
>950 Independence Avenue, S.W.
>Washington, D.C. 20560
>(202) 357-4600

The Museum of African Art is the only museum in the United States dedicated to the collection, exhibition, conservation and study of the arts of Africa South of the Sahara. The museum offers visitors the opportunity to gain a better understanding of the extraordinarily diverse cultural and visual traditions of this vast region.

Since 1979, the museum has engaged in an intensive effort to acquire works of outstanding aesthetic merit, representing the artistic traditions of Africa South of the Sahara. Today, its permanent collection, numbering 6,000 objects, is an excellent resource for the study of African art and culture, jewelry, architectural elements, decorative arts and utilitarian objects. People created the objects in the exhibition whose cultures and traditions are in many respects quite different from those of the western world. In this exhibition, the visitor can see works of art from numerous visual traditions, including those of the Western Sudan Region, the Guinea Coast, Central Africa, East and Southern Africa.

Founded in 1964 in Washington, D.C., by Warren M. Robbins as a private educational institution, the museum of African Art became part of the Smithsonian Institution by an act of Congress in 1979. In 1981, it was renamed the National Museum of African Art. Today, it is both an art museum and a research and reference center. A focal point for the study of the art history and cultures of Africa, the museum exhibits the finest examples of African art and fosters in-depth examination of scholarly topics.

African art is interwoven with daily life in ways quite different from most western art. Religious beliefs find artistic expression not only in the masks and figures created primarily for ceremonial purposes, but in the practical objects of day-to-day existence. A splendid array of sculptures, textiles, household objects, architectural elements, and decorative arts can be found in the museum's collection.

For a variety of reasons, our understanding of art history in Africa is limited. Most African art objects are made from organic materials. They do not last long because they cannot resist the damaging effects of the climate and insects. The relatively few objects that have survived for centuries in Africa are primarily made from stone, terra-cotta, or traditions not seen by outside observers, or if seen, they were not considered to be of enough importance or there was very little information about them. Early written information from the people is lacking as well. Finally, where field evidence is insufficient, scholars and curators often find they are only able to identify objects in a general way according to style or to suggest function by analogy.

Africa is famous for its sculpture in carved wood and ivory, modeled clay, and forged or cast metal. Whether carver, potter, or Smith, an African Artist works with his materials to conceive and produce a three-dimensional work of art.

FLORIDA

Crestview

>The Carver – Hill Museum
>900 Mc Clelland Street
>Crestview, Florida 32536
>(850) 682-4003

Because Jim Crow restricted the education of Blacks and provided for separate but supposedly equal schools for the different races, the Carver – Hill School was created. The Walton County School Board, around 1914, authorized a school for Black children.

The early school operated four months per year. It had several classes in one room and consisted of grades 1-8. In 1968 the school became completely closed as part of the School Integration plan. All of the predominantly Black schools were closed.

The Carver – Hill Alumni Association, to preserve the heritage of the school when it was closed in 1969, created the Carver –Hill Museum and The Carver – Hill Memorial and Historical society, Inc.

The Carver-Hill Alumni Association contacted the Oskaloosa County School Board and asked for a place to preserve the trophies won by Carver – Hill School in sports and academic competitions. Mr. Willie C. Hutchinson appeared before the Board to plead the cause after the integration of schools closed the Carver-Hill School. His request was denied. Contact was made with the Negro Civic Club who still managed the park were the school building stood. They were granted permission for the building to be used for the Carver – Hill Museum. Later, the Council took additional action to designate the building as a museum.

Fort Lauderdale

>Old Dillard Museum
>1009 N.W. fourth St.
>Fort Lauderdale, Florida 33441
>(954) 765 – 6952

"Following in the footsteps of those who came before us, our modern lives reflect the customs of the past. We appreciate the foundations upon which we build today."

Built in 1924, The Old Dillard School, originally called "The Colored School," was not only the first school constructed for Blacks in Broward County, but is also one of the oldest buildings in Fort Lauderdale highlights the significant contributions of the Black community in Broward County. The Old Dillard School renovations were made possible through a cooperative effort between the City of Fort Lauderdale, the School Board of Broward County, the Broward County Commission and the Black Historical Society. The thrust of this effort was to preserve Old Dillard and create a cultural arts education center in which the Old Dillard Museum would be housed in February 1991.

The Old Dillard heritage Gallery has a number of objects that have been donated by community pioneers, elders, and Old Dillard School Alumni Association members. The museum is committed to documenting the "oral traditions" of its peoples" past, home, and abroad.

The Library Resource room offers ethnic reference materials such as books, documents, artifacts, art catalog, films, audio and video tapes, which are at the disposal of museum visitors.

The latest addition to the museum is dedicated to Cannon Adderley – former music instructor at the Old Dillard School. This permanent exhibition houses an interesting collection of photographs and memorabilia of Florida's Jazz Greats. One may observe the history of jazz, its composition arrangement and impact on other cultures. This museum is readily accessible to the physically and mentally challenged.

Miami

Black Archives, History and Research
Foundations of South Florida, Inc. Suite 702
5400 N. W. 22 Ave.
Miami, Florida 33142
(305) 638-6064

Motto: "…Without Vision the People Perish…"

In preparation for the celebration of the United States' two hundredth birthday, Dorothy Jenkins conceived and developed the concept of the Black Archives for South Florida. The Black Archives has become a major resource for historical research in the state of Florida.

The fundamental reason for keeping archives is that they serve as memory. Archives have a dual function: to serve as an essential resource and as evidence of the importance of the collection to the wider community over time.

The Black Archives, History and Research Foundation of South Florida, Inc., is a manuscript/photograph repository. The materials in this repository are collected for educational purposes for users including students, teachers, scholars, researchers, the media, and the public – at large.

The Black Archives Foundation initiated the restoration of several historic sites including the Dr. William A. Chapman, Sr. residence. Located on the campus of Booker T. Washington Middle School, the house was restored for reuse as the Ethnic Heritage Children's Museum. In conjunction with one of Dade County Public School's major goals, Multicultural Education, the Chapman House/ Museum is a district wide multicultural/multiethnic research and museum facility for students of all grade levels to celebrate the rich variety of cultures in Dade County. The program enables students to review the past in relation to the present, and to ponder the possible events of the coming century.

The mission of the Black Archives, History and Research Foundation of South Florida, Inc., is to:

- Operate a repository preserving source materials. The holding includes manuscript, photographs, blueprints, oil paintings and artifacts.
- Provide training and jobs through the creation of a regional tourist "entertainment district" showcasing the legacy of Miami Overtown Community, the era of the Harlem Renaissance, and the character of Black architecture.
- Connect a trail of sites of historical, cultural, and/or architectural significance from the Historic Overtown Folklife Village to the X-Ray clinic and the Chapman House throughout Dade County including Coconut Grove, Railroad Shop, Richmond Heights, Opa Locka, and McFarlane, the black section of Coral Gables.

The trail will continue to sites in Monroe, Broward, Palm Beach counties, and other areas in the state of Florida including Jacksonville, Eatonville and the archaeological site, Ft. Mose, in St. Augustine; and to connect with black heritage trails throughout the Western Hemisphere focusing on ports of call which are historically populated by the "people of color" as defined in 1927 by the Florida Legislature. The Florida Legislature repealed the definition in 1969.

Miami

Black Heritage Museum
Lauren Gail Information
Metro – Park and Recreation Department
P.O. Box 570327
Miami, Florida 33257-0327
(305) 252-3535

The Black Heritage Museum came into existence in May of 1987. Three educators founded it; Mrs. Priscilla Stephens Kruize, Dr. Paul Cadby, and Dr. Earl Wells. These three realized that a multi-ethnic community such as Miami needed a Black Museum, one that represented the cultural heritage of the African-Americans, Jamaicans, Haitians, and other Black groups in the city. Such a museum would stimulate cultural pride within this black community and would promote understanding and racial harmony in the community as a whole.

During its first year, the museum held exhibits in the Model City Cultural Center, the Miami Dade Community College, and the Metropolitan Correctional Center. Lectures and displays were presented at schools, libraries and galleries.

The museum has two purposes, the first being to collect, exhibit and preserve objects and artifacts related to the African – American heritage. Its second objective is to increase community awareness through public exhibits.

An African Proverb: *Unless you call out, who will open the door?*   Ethiopia

Tallahassee

Black Archives Research Center Museum
P.O. Box 809
Florida A & M University
Tallahassee, Florida 32307
904) 599-3020

The purpose of the Black Archives was set forth in an act of the Florida legislature in 1971 which mandated the establishment of a repository to "serve the state by collecting and preserving source material on/or about Black Americans from the earliest beginnings to the present."

The Museum's Mobile Unit

A special service of the archives is its traveling museum, a renovated bus equipped for display offering a selection of museum holdings, including artifacts and tapes.

The Museum's Special Holdings

- The Harriet Tubman Collection
- The Benjamin French Collection
- The S. Randolph Edmonds Collection
- The Neil C. Mooney, Art Consulate State of Florida Department of Education African Art and Artifact Collection
- The Cannonball Adderley Collection
- Don Hill Collection of African memorabilia and artifacts
- Black Americans in Congress Exhibit
- Coon memorabilia

- Jake Gaither films and tapes on football in America
- Official Records of the National Negro Home Demonstration Agent Association

GEORGIA

Atlanta

Apex Museum
135 Auburn Ave. N. E.
Atlanta, Georgia 30303
(404) 581-9813

It was during an evening at a Howard University Alumni banquet in 1978 where Dr. Benjamin Mays was being honored for his years of outstanding service that noted filmmaker Dan Moore crystallized the idea to establish an African-American film archive to celebrate the achievements of unsung African-American heroes like Dr. Mays. The meeting between Dan Moore and Dr. Mays almost immediately resulted in the culmination of the vision and the birth of the Apex.

When Dan Moore discussed the idea of establishing an African-America museum with Mrs. Delores Shelton, she immediately referred him to Mrs. Isabel Gates Webster. A brief meeting with the prominent attorney led to an invitation to meet with attorney Mary Welcome and banker Paul Turner. It was at the initial meeting held at the home of Isabel Webster that the organization was formed and then incorporated in July of 1978.

Throughout all of its years of struggle and challenge, the mission of THE APEX has been to "interpret history from an African-American perspective". Annual visits by thousands, primarily school students, national and international visitors serve as a testament to the need for THE APEX to continue.

Permanent installations in the museum include: the historic Auburn Avenue's Yates & Milton's Drug Store; A Trolley Theater presenting a narration of "Sweet Auburn" history by Cecily Tyson and Julian Bond; a distance learning center for teleconferencing programs donated by Bellsouth; a fine art exhibit area; a gallery for changing exhibits and a gift shop.

Atlanta

The Martin Luther King Jr. Center
For Nonviolent Social Change, Inc.
449 Auburn Avenue, N.E.
Atlanta, Georgia 30312
(404) 524-1956

The Martin Luther King, Jr. Center for Nonviolent Social Change, Inc. is a most unique American institution, totally dedicated to applying the precepts of nonviolence to all areas of human activity.

Martin Luther King, Jr. dedicated his life to teaching and demonstrating that nonviolence is the only viable means to solving man's problems and differences. Today, his commitment lives on at The Martin Luther King, Jr. Center for Nonviolent Social Change. Under the direction of Coretta Scott King, the Center's primary goal is to preserve and advance Dr. King's unfinished mission.

The center is the only official national and international memorial, dedicated to the life and legacy of this man of peace. As you know, Martin Luther King, Jr., was not given the opportunity to complete his work. But the dedicated people at the King Center and its thousands of supporters around the world are working to keep his dream alive.

Almost a million people visit Dr. King's tomb each year. Every one of them is able to serve. To the extent that the King Center can stimulate those hearts and souls to grace and love, we can insure that it does not become a monument to his death, but a touchstone of greatness and life.

Atlanta

Herndon Home
587 University Place, N.W.
Atlanta, Georgia 30314
(404) 581-9813

The Herndon Home is a memorial to the Herndon family, who resided in Atlanta, Georgia from 1910 when it was built by Alonzo Franklin Herndon founder of the Atlanta Life Insurance Company, and his wife Adrienne McNeil, until 1977 when their son Norris Bumstead died. The family's phenomenal achievement was its rise from slavery in Georgia to leadership of the nation's African – American business community. Its tradition of public service and philanthropy contributed substantially to the educational, social, and cultural development of Atlanta. This building, its furnishings and family papers richly document the history of the Herndons and interpret the broad significance of their life and work.

It was a heavy period for Alonzo F. Herndon. Born a Slave in Walton County, Georgia in 1858, he died a millionaire 69 years later in 1927, perhaps the richest black man in America. He made money from barbering, real estate, and the Atlanta Life Insurance Company, The hugely successful firm had been established to be run by and for Blacks.

Despite his limitations (he had one year of formal schooling), Herndon learned to read and write reasonably well, even if he tended to forget the niceties of punctuation. In travels around the world, he collected fine objects of art and often dropped in on favored tailors for his custom suits. Today the 15 room, Beaux Arts Classical – style Herndon Home, designed by Herndon without the help of architects, caps a hilltop on Atlanta's west side as brick legacy overlooking the city.

In recognition of its historical and architectural significance, the Herndon Home is listed in the National Register of Historic Places as part of the Atlanta University Center Historic District. The restoration was completed in 1982.

Atlanta

Lucy Craft Laney Museum of Black History
1116 Phillips Street
Augusta, Georgia 30901
(706) 724-3576

Cassville

Noble Hill – Wheeler Memorial Center
2361 Joe Frank Harris Pkwy
Cassville, Georgia 30123
(770) 382-3392

The Noble Hill – Wheeler Memorial Center is a restored Rosenwald School that was built in 1923 as the first school for Black children. The school was closed in 1955 when Black children began to attend the Bartow Elementary School.

After restoration in 1989, the building now serves as a Black cultural museum that features historical aspects of Black culture in Bartow County, with the primary focus being on lifestyles dating back to the late 1800s.

The museum includes historical information on all schools for Blacks from the early 1900s and more.

The Nobel Hill Center Provides:

- A reflection of Black culture in this area from the late 1800s to the present.
- A small resource library and information on education for Black children from 1923-1955, religious, economic, social and civic activities from the early 1900s.
- A facility which can be used for meetings, luncheons, tours, reunions, class training, small weddings, receptions, showers, picnics, etc.

At the present, there is one building on the Noble Hill site (the Noble Hill Museum), which was completed in the late 1980s. The hope is to continue to develop the Noble Hill site as a historical village, which would include a library, Masonic lodge – country store, etc.

Macon

Harriet Tubman Historical and Cultural Museum
340 Walnut Street
Macon, Georgia 30312
(912) 743-8544

The Harriet Tubman Historical and Cultural Museum was established in 1982 under the guidance of a local Catholic clergyman and a coalition of individuals of various backgrounds who were committed to the development of a facility that would house exhibits depicting the heritage of Afro – Americans, especially those of the Southeast.

Located in a renovated downtown building, the museum houses collections of African arts and Crafts, works by Black artists from across the Southeast, and a library of materials relating to black history. It also serves as a performing arts center and as a meeting place for some local community groups.

One room is dedicated to Tubman herself. Portraits and photographs of the woman looking stern and determined – line a wall near the mural. "She was very compassionate but could also be tough."

The Harriet Tubman Historical and Cultural Museum is housed in a renovated structure that is approximately 8400 square feet. The building consists of four spacious gallery areas. The first includes offices, a main gallery holding the permanent collections, and a mural called "From Africa to America" – seven panel segments each seven feet long depicting the development of the Black American. Also housed in this area is the gift shop where ethnic hand – crafted items and other art objects may be purchased. Adjacent to the gift shop is the east gallery where both the permanent and temporary exhibits are housed.

Madison

Morgan County African American Museum
156 Academy Street
Madison, Georgia 30650
(706) 342- 9191

A new asset to Madison and Morgan Counties is this African – American museum. This museum was a beautifully planned vision shared by Mr. & Mrs. Martin L. Boss. They envisioned this concept of a museum to preserve study and interpret without all the practical trappings needed. They had no money or building, simply their dream. Rev. Alfred Murray, a Morgan County Middle School principal, donated an old house from his property, the Horace Moore house (circa 1895), admittedly an "eyesore to the Boss" dream.

The old house was moved from a vacant lot, to its present location at 156 Academy Street, near Round Bowl Springs. Workers then set about restoring the house for use as a museum. As former state activist, Carroll Hart looked back on her first visit; she describes the house and grounds in this way: "This little house was standing alone in a field with a sad little porch that looked like it might fall any minute." An avalanche of development began to take place; sidewalks were constructed, street resurfaced, drainage system installed, where once unsightly weeds covered the field, flowers now begin to grow. The museum thus stands as a lasting monument to those visionaries whose efforts have come to fruition.

The museum's name was approved by the state of Georgia on October 28, 1991, and was awarded a grant of $9,500 by Governor Zell Miller from his discretionary fund.

Currently the museum consists of:
- A living room with period furniture
- Morgan County Room (providing seminars on the people and their history)
- An African Room (housing African paintings and exhibits)
- A Reference Library

Milledgeville

Sallie Ellis Davis House
301 South Clark Street
Milledgeville, Georgia 31061-3343
(912) 452-0268

In 1990, the Sallie Ellis Davis Foundation, Inc. was formed by a group of Milledgeville citizens to promote an awareness of Black history in Milledgeville. The group immediately began to pursue the rehabilitation of the Sallie Ellis Davis House at 301 South Clark Street.

Who was Sallie Ellis Davis? Sallie Ellis Davis was born outside Milledgeville in Baldwin County, Georgia, in the mid 1870s to Josh Ellis and Elizabeth Brunswick. As a young girl, Sallie was sent for a primary and secondary education with other children of Baldwin County. Early on she expressed a commitment to education and a desire to teach. In the mid 1890s, she enrolled in Atlanta University's Normal School. As a student at Atlanta University, Sallie Ellis was taught and strongly influenced by one of the most significant minds of early 20th century America, Dr. W. E. B. DuBois. It was Dr. DuBois' philosophy of education, one that exposed the enrichment of the total being that Sallie Ellis carried with her into the classroom, and throughout her life. Dr. DuBois continued to serve as her friend and mentor as Sallie Ellis began her career as a math teacher and administrator at the Eddy School in Milledgeville.

The Sallie Ellis Davis House will be used as a local museum and small meeting facility. The existing central hall will remain in tact. The four major rooms will accommodate reception type functions. These rooms will also contain a few exhibit panels to illustrate the important associations of this house with Sallie Ellis Davis.

Savannah

King – Tisdell Cottage
502 East Harris Street
Savannah, Georgia 31401
(912) 234-8000

The Beach Institute at 502 East Harris Street, in downtown Savannah, houses the offices of the King – Cottage Foundation, Inc., and the Ulysses Davis Collection and frequent exhibits.

Built in 1867 by the Freedmen's Bureau, the project was primarily funded by the American Missionary Association. It was named in honor of New York Alfred Eli Beach, editor of Scientific

American Magazine and inventor of the typewriter and the first New York City subway system Mr. Beach donated the funds to purchase the land.

The Beach Institute was founded in 1867 as a school for African Americans. It was the first school opened in Savannah, Georgia specifically for the education of African Americans after the abolishment of slavery.

Initially there were 600 enrolled students, 9 female teachers and a male principal. Most of these teachers were White. Tuition at that time was $1 per month.

In 1874, The Beach Institute was turned over to the Savannah Board of Education and became a <u>free</u> public school for Black children.

In 1874, the school was damaged by fire rendering it temporarily unusable. The American Missionary Association took this opportunity to resume control of the building and the educational program, as they were intent on securing a higher grade of instruction than Savannah's Board of Education thought prudent to furnish.

In 1917, the Savannah Boys Club rented one small room in the basement of the Beach Institute as its weekly meeting place. The activities and fame of the club extended and expanded until it occupied the entire basement of the building and utilized every weekday evening with its educational endeavors on behalf of the under – privileged Negro boys.

Enrollment significantly declined due to the opening of Savannah's first Black public high school on Cuyler Street, as well as the prevailing popularity of the Georgia State Industrial College at Thunderbolt, which opened in 1891, now called Savannah State University. The Beach Institute closed in 1919.

Savannah

Ralph Mark Gilbert Civil Rights Museum
460 Martin Luther King Jr. Blvd.
Savannah, Georgia 31401
(912) 231-8900

The Ralph Mark Gilbert Civil Rights Museum, recently named "Georgia's Best New History Museum" by the Georgia Journal, chronicles the civil rights struggle of Georgia's oldest African-American community from slavery to the present.

The Museum is located in historic Savannah in a five level building erected in 1914 as the Wage Earners Savings and Loan Bank for Black Savannahians, which was the largest Black bank in the county at that time.

The Ralph Mark Gilbert Civil Rights Museum is named in honor of the late Dr. Ralph Mark Gilbert, father of Savannah's civil rights movement and fearless NAACP leader. He was known for much more than his outspoken campaigns for civil rights. He was a nationally known orator, pulpiteer and playwright, producing religious dramas (passion plays) throughout the country.

Dr. Gilbert served as pastor of historic First African Baptist Church in Savannah for 16 years. In 1942 he reorganized the Savannah branch of the NAACP, served as president for eight years, and convened the first state conference where he was elected president. Under his courageous leadership, more than forty NAACP branches were organized in Georgia by 1950.

His tenure as president was marked by significant contributions for equality and justice in Georgia. He led the fight to end the White Democratic Primary, launched a citywide voter registration drive that registered hundreds of Black voters in Savannah, and removed boss rule in local politics. His support for a reform mayor and council slate, led to integration of law enforcement in Georgia in 1947 when nine Black policemen were hired in Savannah. Dr. Ralph Mark Gilbert died in 1956, leaving a legacy of outstanding leadership in Savannah and throughout Georgia.

IDAHO

Idaho

Idaho Black History Museum
508 Julia Drive
Boise, Idaho 83702
(208) 433-0017

The Idaho Black History Museum's permanent exhibit depicts the 196-year history of African-Americans in Idaho beginning with York, a slave who was part of the Lewis and Clark Expedition in 1805 to Boise's own musical genius Gene Harris. Through photographs, artifacts and oral history, Idaho Black History Museum's permanent exhibition examines the establishment of Idaho's Black community focusing on employment trends, the arts, discrimination issues, and cultural traditions.

(IBHM) is developing three projects that make up the long-range plan for the museum. The first is permanent exhibitions. The second project is the development and distribution of curriculum on Idaho Black History. The final phase will be the development of an exhibit that will travel the state and educate the community about Idaho's diverse history.

The creation and installation of the permanent exhibition will bring Idaho's Black history to life. The permanent exhibition will employ a variety of low-and high-tech methods to communicate Idaho's rich history with its visitors including informative text-based displays, images, a resource area, an interactive website, audio tapes of oral histories, video images and more.

The permanent exhibition will enable individuals of all ages, races, and economic backgrounds to make personal connections with Idaho's Black history and learn more about individuals, events and facts that are unique to the State of Idaho, such as:

- York, a slave, was the first Black person to travel through Idaho as part of the Lewis and 'Clark Expedition in 1805.
- Some of the earliest Black settlers in Idaho were Mormons who had come to Utah with Brigham Young in 1847 and eventually settled in Eastern Idaho.
- Elvina Moulton, a former slave, became a charter member of the Boise Presbyterian Church in 1878.
- The St. Paul Baptist church building, one of the last remaining structures built by all Black labor that now houses the Idaho Black History Museum, was built in 1921.

Idaho held its first civil rights rally in 1968 after the assassination of Dr. Martin Luther King, Jr.

ILLINOIS

Chicago

Carter G. Woodson Regional Library
Vivian Harsh Collection of
Afro – American History and Literature
9525 South Halsted Street
Chicago, Illinois 60628
(312) 745-2080

The largest African-American history and literature collection in the Midwest had its humble start with Vivian G. Harsh. She was born in Chicago in the year 1890 and died in 1960. Mrs. Harsh attended an African-American high school -Wendell Phillips which is located on Chicago' south side and Fisk University in Tennessee. After graduating from Fisk University, she returned to Chicago's south side to work for the Chicago Public Library System for the balance of her life. Vivian became the first Black librarian in the Chicago Public Libraries. Working at the George Cleveland Hall branch, Harsh started a Black history collection with funding from the Rosenwald Foundation Grants, donations from patrons and her own purchases. The library system administration did not believe public funds should be spent on this project. As the collection grew, the reputation spread. The branch became a meeting place for young Black writers and artists.

Harsh encouraged young writers to help build the Black collection at the branch. She was called "the lieutenant" by some of her colleagues and a taskmaster by many of the youth who did their research at the branch. She was eulogized as "the historian who never wrote" (Slaughter 1960), yet she succeeded in building one of the most important research collections on Black history and literature in the Midwest.

In 1975, the collection was moved to a new and larger building at 95th and Halsted with the name Carter G. Woodson Regional Library. The Harsh collection was housed in the north wing and this section renamed the Vivian G. Harsh Research Collection. In recent years, this collection has outgrown the present space because of the volumes of Black History material. With the help of the society for the Advancement of the Vivian G. Harsh Research Collection of Afro-American History and Literature, adjacent land was purchased for additional space to adequately assist with the growth of materials and researchers using the collection.

Chicago Malcolm X College
1900 West Van Buren Street
Chicago, Illinois 60612
312/942-3000

College History

Malcolm X College is a contemporary-style building of black steel and glass. The present-day Malcolm X College has a long and glorious history. The first of the City Colleges of Chicago, the school was founded in 1911 and was known as Crane Junior College and Herzel Junior College. The school has been located at many different sites, although always on the city's west side. Malcolm X College strives to bring to reality the dreams of the man whose name it bears: *"Education is an important element in the struggle for human rights. It is the means to help our children and people rediscover their identity and thereby increase self-respect. Education is our passport to the future, for tomorrow belongs to those who prepares for it today."*

Artifacts at Malcolm X College

The college houses many unique and interesting pieces of art, which are outstanding, and enhances the beauty of the building.

1st Fl. Van Buren and Jackson Corridors. The glass-enclosed sculptures are replicas of part of the Malvina Hoffman collection. "The Races of Mankind", on loan from the Field Museum. The names and geographical locations of the peoples depicted are as follows:

Van Buren Corridor (east to west).
- Ituri Forest Pygmies - Central Africa.
- Kalahari Bushman - Kalahari Desert, Southwest Africa.
- Solomon Islander - Solomon Islands, Southwest Pacific Ocean.
- Semang Pygmy - Malaysia, Southeast Asia, Pacific Ocean.

Cross Corridor (west end).
Shabazz Study Hall.
- The three wood carved panels on the west wall are from Dar es Salaam, Tanzania, East Africa.
- The black and white photographic exhibit of "Great Black Women in Contemporary African-American History" was executed by Dorothea Jacobson, a Malcolm X instructor of photography. She has also included the portrait of Sojourner Truth, Black abolitionist.
- South Wall - green, white and brown framed tie-dye - East Africa. The companion piece is in Room 1200.

President's Complex. (Room 1100)
- West Wall - framed official commemorative textile from United Nations Decade of Women's Conference held in 1985, Nairobi, Kenya.

Just south of Room 1100 is the glass enclosed bronze bust of MALCOLM X. On the east wall (centered) is a hand-woven KENTE CLOTH from Accra, Ghana. (1972). "Of the regalia of Ghanaian chiefs, particularly those of Southern Ghana, there is no part more distinctive than their ceremonial dress. The most notable item, of course, is the silk-woven Kente cloth. The uniqueness of the Kente lies not only in the artistry of its manufacture but also in the manner in which it is worn and the regal dignity it confers on the wearer."

(PANOPLY OF GHANA), by A.A.Y. Kyerematen, Room 1200: Framed tie-dyes, Paaya Pa Gallery, Nairobi, Kenya

Jackson Corridor (west to east)
- Mangbetu Woman - Zaire, Central Africa.
- Sudan Woman - from the grasslands area that stretches from west to east Africa - south of the Sahara Desert.
- Zulu Woman - Zulu society, South Africa.
- Ubangi Woman - Congo Republic, West Central Africa.
- Centered in this corridor is the last automobile of MALCOLM X.

Cross Corridor (east end).
African American Cultural Center.
- Nuer Warrior - Nuer Society, Northeast Africa.
- Warrior (with spear and shields), "Black Man", from the "Unity of Mankind" section of the Hoffman Collection. This is a symbolic figure.
- Sara Girl - Sara Society, francophone area, equatorial (central) Africa.
- West African sculpture in the cabinet with an orange background.
- Hand-woven and embroidered green shama - Ethiopia, Northeast Africa.
- Black and White Kente shawl - Ghana, West Africa.

The carvings in the above two cases are Makonde from East Africa.
Robert Witter, Professor of Art, Malcolm X College executed the two modern sculptures centered on the east wall.

***Room 1200 (Conference Room A) also contains five metal sculptures representing the world's great religions: Christianity, Islam, Judaism, Taoism, and Hinduism.

2nd Fl. The Carter G. Woodson Library

The library was named after "The Father of Black History," the historian who organized The Association for the Study of Black Life and History (1915, Chicago), and who initiated Black History Week in 1926. His portrait, along with that of MALCOLM X, hangs on the south wall.

The two large ebony sculptures on pedestals are Makonde, from National Arts of Tanzania, Dar es Salaam. Craftsmen who inhabit the border areas of Tanzania and Mozambique did these original carvings.

Jackson Corridor (west to east) WALL MURALS.

- To the right of office 2217: an unfinished figure by Charles Dawson.
- To the right of office 2218 is a depiction of "the first man and woman". There are a number of symbols surrounding the central figures.
- Between offices 2233 and 2234 is an unfinished mural of protest against police brutality.
- To the left of Room 2239 is a mural of Hispanic creativity. The Taino were Arawakan Indians of Hispaniola (now Haiti and the Dominican Republic in the Caribbean.) These Indians became extinct after the Spanish conquest. It may be assumed that "The Cemi" was a mythological god.

Exterior of the building - Van Buren Street

The free form structure west of the main entrance displays several original "Walls of Respect" which were created by Black artists during the 60's and early 70's. This new art form was found on the walls of buildings and viaducts. It was basically protest in nature. It also focused on the problems that beset the Black community in its struggle against racism and oppression, as do the MURALED DOORS in the interior of the college. These doors, unique in their beauty and design, confront the viewer with their powerful messages. Eugene Edaw, professor of art, Kennedy-King College, executed them.

Chicago

> DuSable Museum of African History
> 740 East 56th Place
> Chicago, Illinois 60637
> 312/947-0600

MOTTO: *"The seed is sown"*

Founded in 1961, the DuSable Museum hosted eight exhibitions. It is the first non-profit museum dedicated to the history, art culture of African-Americans in the Midwest.

As an institution representative of so many firsts in the Black community, DuSable Museum takes its name in honor of an African-American who is synonymous with firsts - Jean Baptiste Pointe DuSable. DuSable was a Haitian pioneer of mixed African and European parentage. He came to the United States in 1764 and in 1770 he became the first non-Indian settler in the area that became Chicago.

The Museum's purpose is to preserve, interpret and display the rich heritage embodied in African and African-American history, literature, art, language, and material culture.

History

The DuSable Museum of African-American History is the major independent institution in Chicago established to preserve and interpret the historical experiences and achievements of African Americans. During the 30-year existence it has become a national leader among the 150 or more African American museums in the U.S.A. The DuSable Museum is unique in its origin and is a vital part of Chicago's cultural community.

The Museum is proud of its diverse holdings that number well over 10,000 pieces and include paintings, sculpture, print works and historical memorabilia. Specific artists, historic events or collections on loan from individuals or institutions feature special exhibitions, workshops and lectures to highlight works.

The DuSable Museum is located in Chicago, a city rich in African-American history. The first outsider to settle in the area in the 1770's was a Black fur trader named Jean Baptiste Pointe DuSable. He built a permanent settlement and developed a friendly working relationship with the Indian communities, the Pottawatomi, Iroquois, Oneida, and others.

Nearly 150 years later, a Black history movement was founded in Chicago. Dr. Carter G. Woodson convened a conference in Chicago in 1915 to found the Association for the Study of Negro Life and History. The Black community of Chicago organized its Black history movement around this new organization, along with key intellectual and cultural leaders.

One of the principal figures to emerge after World War II was Margaret Burroughs. She was educated at the Art Institute of Chicago, and taught art at DuSable High School. Burroughs came from a family of activists and continued in their tradition. In the 1940s, she established with others, the National Negro Museum and Historical Foundation. In 1959, she joined a group of artists to found an important national organization, the National Conference of Negro Artists, now known as the National Conference of Artists. In 1961, she founded, in her home, the institution now known as the DuSable Museum of African American History.

The Early Years

Founding members of the museum taught Black history in the community. In addition to Margaret Burroughs, there were several other key figures: Charles Burroughs, a published poet and a heroic fighter for freedom and democracy, who volunteered to fight against fascism in Spain in the 1930s by joining the Abraham Lincoln Brigade; Gerard Lew, a postal clerk and poet, whose ancestors had fought in the American Revolutionary War; Ralph Turner worked for the railroad and became a community lecturer in Black history; and Eugene Feldman, educated as a journalist and the author of several popular works on Black History.

The first location of DuSable Museum, 3806 South Michigan Avenue was the former family home of John Griffith, a major Chicago contractor. It was converted to the Quincy Club, a boarding room facility for railroad workers. Ralph Turner helped arrange for the house to be purchased for the Museum when the Quincy Club declined. The new museum was chartered in February 1961 and opened its door on October 21st of that year.

During the first year, over 2500 visitors viewed eight exhibits. This was the only place in the city of Chicago to learn about Black history, from ancient African to current events. The museum was supported by a wide range of organizations, especially schools, youth groups (YMCA and YWCA, Scouts, workshops in art and writing, etc.) and the local membership of organizations like the Association for the Study of Negro Life and History and the National Conference of Artists.

As the museum evolved, it experienced several name changes starting with the Ebony Museum of Negro History and Art and, in 1966 changing to the Museum of African American History and Art. In 1968, it was renamed the DuSable Museum of African-American History to honor Chicago's first settler.

With the museum's holdings increasing steadily, the founders soon saw the need for larger quarters. In 1971, the Chicago Park District granted the museum permission to use a former administration building in Washington Park of the city's South Side.

The move into new facilities brought about many positive changes for the DuSable Museum including a full-time professional staff, greater recognition throughout the large community, increased exhibition gallery space and public education programs. The expanded space also led to larger numbers of visitors and more programs for all segments of the community.

Since its founding, the DuSable Museum, regarded by its peers as a leader in the development of African-American museums, has continued its efforts to refine and expand programs, collections, services and gain even broader recognition in the museum community.

The DuSable Museum continues as a dynamic institution. Its traditions link the museum to the Black community of its origin where tens of thousands of youth are provided their first exposure to Black history. Its presence reinforces and stimulates the cultural life of the Black community while enriching the awareness of Black life and culture by the total community.

INDIANA

Indiana

Crispus Attucks High School Museum
1140 Martin Luther King
Indianapolis, Indiana 46202
(317) 226-4613

The Crispus Attucks Museum is one component of the Crispus Attucks Center of African Centered / Multicultural Education. The Center is under the auspices of the Indianapolis Public School system. The mission for the center is to act as a catalyst of knowledge for teaching, learning and understanding the experiences of Africans, African American, people of color and other ethnic and cultural groups, and the vital role these experiences have played in the development of world civilizations.

The Crispus Attucks Museum was established to recognize, honor and celebrate the outstanding contributions made by African Americans and more especially, Crispus Attucks High School graduates. It will provide an accurate documentation of historic events through research, exhibits and demonstrations. If you are not from Indianapolis just mention Crispus Attucks High School, and a long conversation is started. Crispus Attucks High School has had a shining history in sports, music, and educating students. Attucks produced three state champion basketball teams in 1955, 1956 and 1959. The school was remembered for its dedicated instruction. Marian Kurtz president, of the1944 class said," We had black history in Attucks everyday," Kurtz said, "It was instilled in us, dignity, heritage, and culture."

The story of Crispus Attucks High School is a vital part of the local struggle for equality in the 20th century. Crispus Attucks was created during a period of intense racism and injustice that was manifest in many overt acts of discrimination throughout the United States. Indianapolis was not immune from the pernicious doctrine of segregation and inequality. "Negro children" were allowed to attend Indianapolis high schools on an integrated basis from 1877 to 1927. However, a "Ku Klux Klan inspired petition in 1922 brought about a resolution from the Indianapolis Board of School Trustees, which authorized the creation of a "colored high school". With such school, "Negro students" through Indianapolis were up – rooted from their high schools and forced to attend Crispus Attucks High School.

Gilbert L. Taylor a graduate of Attucks and the curator of the Crispus Attucks Center Museum tells us the three purposes of the museum are to reflect the history of African Americans who are graduates of Attucks and citizens of the world; to provide accurate documentation about the history, tradition, culture and values of African Americans. The last objective is to provide the Indianapolis community with a permanent site for housing African American artifacts and especially those pertaining to Crispus Attucks.

Kansas

Wichita

> First National Black Historical
> Society of Kansas
> 501 N. Water
> P.O. Box 2695
> Wichita, Kansas 67201
> 316/262-7651
> 316/686-6847
> Founded November 1973

The pride of a group is exemplified by reflections of its past, yet, all too often the involvement and contributions of Black Americans are buried or omitted form the annals of history.

Based on this concept, the First National Black Historical Society of Kansas which originated in the minds of five Black women (Doris Kerr-Larkin, Barbara Ann Kerr, Ra 'Shualoama Beruni, Carolyn J. Myeres, and Decker Mae Alford) had served as a center for Black Life for more than half a century at that time. They believed that the building qualified as a historical landmark and was sufficiently appointed to be used as a museum for Black History in Wichita.

African-Americans who came to Wichita shortly after the Civil War and during the first decade of its establishment as a city, settled in the vicinity of the 500 and 600 blocks of North Main. By 1880, approximately two dozen families had arrived and expansion included the adjacent streets, North Water and North Wichita. Total social, business and religious life of Blacks was highly concentrated along these three streets. At the turn of the century, the total population was 25,000 with six percent being Black residents. Although they were small in percentage, the Black provided considerable significance.

The Museum and Cultural Center was established in 1983 to give recognition to Black participation in early Wichita.

Programs
- Genealogy
- Black Kansas Archivers
- Buffalo Soldier
- African Artifacts

Louisiana

New Orleans

> The Amistad Research Center
> Tulane University-Tilton Hall
> New Orleans, Louisiana 70118-5698
> 504/865-5535

Amistad is among the largest of the nation's repositories specializing in the history of Afro-Americans. Papers of Black Americans and records of organizations and institutions of the Black community make up about 90 percent of the Center's holdings.

The Amistad Adventure

On the morning of June 28, 1839, La Amistad (The Friendship) set sail from Havana, beginning an adventure of far-reaching historical consequences. On board the little schooner were 53 Africans who had been abducted from West Africa and sold in violation of international law. Their intended fate was enslavement on plantations down coast from Havana.

On the third day out, led by one Cinque, the Africans revolted and ordered that the ship be guided toward the rising sun, back to Africa, but each night the Cubans reversed direction. Zigzagging for two months, the ship eventually was brought by northerly winds and currents to Long Island. The Africans were jailed and charged with piracy and murder.

In New York City, a group of Christian abolitionists, headed by Lewis Tappan, formed a defense committee. Attorneys, with help from former President John Quincy Adams, took the case to the United States Supreme Court, which rules that the Africans were free. The Amistad Committee evolved into the inter-racial American Missionary Association (A.M.A.), which since then has been in the forefront of the fight for freedom and justice. The A.M.A. founded hundreds of abolitionist and anti-caste churches and schools among Black Americans, Native Americans, Puerto Ricans, Appalachian Whites, Asian Americans, and Chicanos. Distinguished colleges and universities that emerged from these efforts include Atlanta, Berea, Dillard, Fisk, Hampton, Huston-Tillotson, Le Moyne - Owen, Piedmont, Talladega, and Tougaloo.

MARYLAND

Baltimore

    Morgan State University
    Morris A. Soper Library
    Davis Special Collections
    Cold Spring Lane & Hillen Road
    Baltimore, Maryland 21239

Beulah Myrtle - Davis built Morgan University library. Miss Davis' energy spills over into what is now known as the Beulah Myrtle Davis Special Collections.

It is a full-fledge museum of archives consisting of books, manuscripts, educationally, sociologically and scientifically inventive Blacks. The Davis room is a gold mine of Afro-American history

Cambridge

    Stanley Institute & Christ Rock
    Route 16 and Bayley Road
    Cambridge, Maryland 21613-1199

Two and a half miles southwest of the Cambridge Court House, on Church Creek Road, near the cross-roads of Bayley and Dailsville, was once a big, big rock; almost a boulder. Most men of this community would often say, "I'll meet you at the rock". The rock became the place to talk about future plans, shucking, oysters, shooting matches, and whatever else interesting that might come up.

When the Church was built near this rock, they then would say, "Lets go out to Christ Rock." At this time, every one who lived in this area was related to each other totaling about eighty families. This area was eventually called Christ Rock.

There was an addition to this pious community of Christ Rock in 1867. Ezekiel Stanley and Moses Opher moved a small building from a site near Church Creek, Maryland. This building was to be the community school house. The people, who assisted with this moving, wanted an elaborate name for the school. They decided to honor Ezekiel Stanley, so the school was named Stanley Institute. It was a one room structure which was approximately 30' x 24' x 12'. At one period in time, the student enrollment was so high as eighty five, with the grades ranging from one through seven. By the time the school closed its doors to student enrollment in 1962, the highest grade level was six.

The Stanley Institute was the first community owned school in Dorchester County. It served two purposes at one point, church and school until 1875.

In 1966 when the school was closed to all students, William H. Kiah changed the P.T.A. to Rock Community Improvement League. This League was organized to improve the community and the building. The building was to serve two purposes at this time; number one - to have early 1900 furniture, books, etc. - the league felt that in restoring this building with the turn of the century furniture and books, the heritage of that era in education would not be lost; number two - was to have artifacts, pictures, and collectibles on hand to educate all on Black America's past and present.

The league feels that a museum of Black History will encourage modern history of the community. For a long time, education was the main kingdom - the route to liberation for Black Americans, and then came the political and social kingdom. Now it is the culture kingdom.

Culture embraces religion, life, styles, heritage and all the questions that have to do with being. Museums are a way to not only say, but also show who you are. The goals of the league consists mainly of making Black Americans more aware of their History.

Hagerstown

> Marguente Doleman House Museum
> 54019 Locust Street
> Hagerstown, Maryland 21740
> 301-739-8185
> Founded 1975

This is a guest house museum started by Marguente Doleman. She founded it in 1975. It mainly deals with Afro-American history memorabilia. There are five rooms filled with various artifacts that she has collected over the years. If you want to see the items call for an appointment 1-301-739-8185.

Artifacts

Books on Washington County	Pencils
75 buttons	Caribbean Island
Maryland 1860 to 1870	300 books on Blacks
Match box covers	100 post cards
Book on property owners	Dolls
Kitchen utilities	Clothing

MASSACHUSETTS

Boston

Museum of Afro-American History
46 Joy Street
Boston, Massachusetts 02114
617/742-1854

They called it the Abolitionist Church, The Black Faneuil Hall. They called it a sanctuary, a center for civil disobedience, a rallying point for military volunteers. For nearly a century, the African Meeting House was a moral center for the Black community on Beacon Hill.

By the 1800's, 1,100 Bostonians made up the largest free Black community in North America. Most black Bostonians lived in a crowded, rundown area called the North End. Some worked as dock workers, street laborers and many were servants.

Blacks in Boston were concerned with establishing strong independent organizations, with educating their children, and with working to end slavery throughout the nation. In 1806, they built what is now the oldest standing Black building in the nation - the African Meeting House.

The African Meeting House was a focus of Boston's Black community. A center for religious, politics and social activity, the building served as a church, a meeting hall, and often as a residence, as well.

Here Frederick Douglass, Wendell Phillips and Charles Summer spoke in defense of human rights. Maria W. Stewart delivered her historic defense of women's rights in the early 1830s from the Meeting House podium. Members of the historic Massachusetts 54th Regiment of Black Civil War Soldiers enlisted at the Meeting House.

In reaction to the Fugitive Slave Law of 1850, Black Bostonians developed a network of "safe" houses on the north slope of the hill. The community provided refuge to escaped slaves, seeing them safely to freedom on the Underground Railroad.

At the end of the 19th century when the Black community began to migrate to the South End and Roxbury sections of Boston, the Meeting House was sold to a Jewish organization and remained a synagogue until it was purchased by the Museum of African-American. It closed for a time and reopened the African Meeting House on October 11, 1987.

Boston's small 19th century community of Black citizens made great accomplishments under devastating circumstances. They built a foundation not only for their race but also for their country. Their day-to-day activities, their struggle for equal rights, their concern for their neighbors, and their courage have been captured and preserves in the hearts and minds of their descendants through literature, the arts, and in buildings that stand as movements to their dedication to freedom.

The types of program offered:

- Special events of music, literature, visual and performing arts.
- Exhibits that offer little known facts about African American Life in New England from 1638 to the present.

MICHIGAN

Detroit

Your Heritage House
110 East Ferry Avenue
Detroit, Michigan 48202
313/871-1667

Your Heritage House is both a museum and fine arts center for youth. In practice and philosophy it is an adventure and exploration in the fine and lively arts. The founders of Your Heritage House many years ago saw the need for a place where children could be comfortable with the fine arts, with their own cultural heritage and share in the heritage of others. Black heritage was the keystone around which a broader philosophy of universal heritage was constructed.

Your Heritage House was established in July 1969. Its founder, Gwendolyn Harkless Hogue and Josephine Harreld Love, with awareness of the discouraging prophecies regarding large cities and particularly Detroit, set about to plant within its core their expression of faith in the ability of human beings

At its founding the principal asset of Your Heritage House was a collection of child-related fine art, literature, and objects assembled by Josephine Love. Children were then, as now, granted easy access to materials usually ordained for locked showcases.

Today's collection has been expanded through numerous gifts, often acquired by friends in their travels. Recently, a Catholic nun, assigned to the Hope Ship, carried fragile terra cotta figures purchased from village artisans by knapsack from Northern Brazil in a circuitous route to Detroit.

Manuscripts scores recordings and assorted published and unpublished materials line the walls. Books for and about children include such topics as art and architecture, crafts, folklore, music, and the media. Josephine Love selected a unique collection of music for children. A wide selection of materials relating to Black heritage includes folk tales, field recordings, handcrafts and household objects fashioned by village artisans in Africa.

The artist is represented in the museum by paintings, graphics and sculpture. These include soft-sculpture figures by Detroit's Christine Baker, which depict various peoples of the African nations - Masai, Watusi, Zulu, Makemba.

Detroit

Graystone International Jazz Museum   (CLOSED)
3000 East Grand Blvd.
Detroit, Michigan 48202
313/871-0234

Founded in May of 1974, the Graystone International Jazz Museum serves as a repository of Jazz memorabilia, which documents the history of improvisational music and the musicians who are its creators. The Museum promotes and conducts research which traces the development of improvisation from its beginning in traditional African rhythms to its innovative maturation in American-African forms and styles.

Recognizing the influence American-African improvisation has had on music in the United States and abroad, the Graystone International Jazz Museum had adopted a cultural-historical approach to the study and presentation of improvisational music - that which is called "Jazz" and all of the other classification of American-African music. This approach takes into account not only the African heritage of improvisation, but also the subsequent adoption of the resultant musical styles and rhythm patterns by musicians almost worldwide.

When we speak of Detroit, a poorly documented history indicates that Jazz was slow in getting started, but grew to be a rich institution. As early as 1857, a gifted and versatile black musician named Theodore Finney co-led a band on a steamer traveling between Detroit, Michigan and Sandusky, Ohio. The music was the earliest to be associated with the sound of jazz, although it could be more accurately described as march music.

The Graystone-Jazz Museum lives as an institution founded by James T. Jenkins to gather artifacts, to foster-research and oral history and to carry forward year-a-round the best of the living jazz forms through concerts and outreach programs. The significance is incalculable in terms of its value in stimulating the intellect of our youth, sustaining the heritage of our adults and supporting our artists. Moreover, this truly special kind of music serves as a creative catalyst, encouraging humanity to seek a path for a positive and promising future.

Detroit

Motown Museum
Hitsville U.S.A.
2648 West Grand Blvd.
Detroit, Michigan 48208
313/ 875-2264

Barry Gordy's sister, Esther Edwards, recalls, "His friends asked, 'you're going to quit?' They thought he was crazy." Barry Gordy at 29 years old quit his assembly line worker job at Ford to make records.

Welcome to the Motown-Museum at Hitsville, U.S.A., the house that changed the outlook and sound of the musical world. At a time when rock 'n roll was taking over the airwaves of America, there was a different sound coming from this small home at 2648 West Grand rhythmic and distinctive..."The Motown Sound".

In January of 1959, Berry Gordy, Jr. purchased this house with an $800 loan from the Berry Co-op, the family savings club. He christened the house "Hitsville U.S.A.," and hung a shingle out front. As Motown grew, Gordy bought seven more houses on the block to accommodate the different divisions of the company. In 1968, Motown moved its headquarters to 2457 Woodward Avenue in downtown Detroit, but the artists continued to record at Hitsville until Motown moved its headquarters to Hollywood, California in 1972. The Detroit Motown office operated out of Hitsville until it became the Motown Museum in 1988. A visit to the Motown Historical Museum gives everyone an opportunity to see where the music and stars of Motown began. People from all over the world come to this small, but very special house to see the original Studio A where the sounds of Motown were first recorded. It still looks as though a recording session is about to begin.

Gordy coined the word Motown in 1960, by condensing the words "motor" and "town" because he wanted his company name to reflect his hometown of Detroit. In 1982, the word Motown was incorporated into Webster's New World Dictionary of the American Language. Today, Detroit is known as Motown all over the world.

One of the largest exhibits is the Michael Jackson Room dedicated to one of the most phenomenal stars in the world history. "How sweet it is."

Detroit
        Concept East II   (CLOSED)
        The Black Cinema Gallery
        1144 Pingree
        Detroit, Michigan 48202
        313-972-1030

James Wheeler, a free-lance photographer and self-made archivist, created Concept East II as a combination movie house and learning arena for lovers of Black film memorabilia. Historians regard Wheeler's collection as among the best in the nation and he is considered a leading authority on black films.

"I never really thought a lot of people were preserving a part of black history," said Wheeler, explaining his motivation. "Black cinema is virtually lost and ignored by film historians and Black culture researchers. It's tragic that people don't know that between 1910 and 1950 over 350 to 400 all-Black films were made." Since 1953, Wheeler has compiled 300 classic films, numerous cartoon, photographs and more than 1,000 original movie posters featuring black performers and caricatures.

"One of my dreams is to open a Black Hollywood Museum."

There are many new Black filmmakers out there whose work is seldom, if ever, seen. Hence, another function of Concept East II and the Black Cinema Gallery are to provide this much needed outlet. Some of Wheeler's favorite old movies are the films by Oscar Micheaux, a black producer and director who made 40 films between 1916 and 1940.

Wheeler would like to have an on-going archives where people can view and study black films - a real theater, a real museum with the proper lighting and displays.

"But no one enter a strong man's house and plunder his goods, unless he first binds the strong man; then indeed he may plunder his house" (Mark 3:27).

Flint
        Greater Flint Afro-American
        Hall of Fame, Inc.
        36 Pingree
        Flint, Michigan 48503
        (313) 743-8795
        President, Norman Bryant
        Secretary, Robin Fields
        Founded October 1983

During the first week in September, Norman Bryant told his wife he was going over to Max Brandon's house for a few minutes to share with him an idea he had about starting a Hall of Fame for Black Athletes from the Flint area. Max and Norman got so engrossed in the idea that they talked at least four hours about the subject. After that meeting, Norman decided to call the first meeting to organize the Hall of Fame Committee.

The goal is to preserve and exhibit the history of former Flint Afro-American professional, semi-professional, college, city, high school, sandlot players, and teams from as early as possible to an undetermined date.

CRITERIA FOR SELECTION OF INDUCTEES

The Greater Flint Afro-American Hall of Fame Selection Committee is responsible for obtaining written, documented historical background of each candidate for admission to the Hall of Fame.

Information is based on documented, recorded individual records of performance such as school year - books, newspaper articles, magazines, media tapes, films, etc. An individuals' performance is not based on team records. Team performances are attributed to managers and coaches.

Detroit

>National Afro-American Sports
>Hall of Fame and Gallery
>P.O. Box 27615
>Detroit, Michigan 48227
>(313) 571-4444
>Founder Elmer Anderson
>Co Founder Art Finney
>Founded January 9, 1982

In December 1977, Elmer Anderson approached Art Finney, editor of a union paper, with the idea of writing articles about former sports players than working in the shops. This was done, and together toward this goal, Elmer and Art got people at the first organization meeting.

This charter group debated the need for a hall and was generally agreeable on the following. The history of Blacks in sports from the mid 1800s to 1960 was fast disappearing and there was to our knowledge, no one place where much of it was preserved. It exists in old, mainly Black oriented newspapers and magazines: in scrapbooks and memorabilia of old-time Black athletes or with their families or friends, and also in the memories of the participants. As these persons pass on, first hand accounts die with them.

It is fitting and deserving for the Afro-American to have this rich lore of sports history preserved for them and their posterity. It will show that Blacks did achieve equal to, and in some cases out-achieve the athletes with whom they were allowed to compete with for over fifty years. (The Hall's temporary home is on the fourth floor of the Wayne County Building, 600 Randolph, Detroit, Michigan.)

Inductees

1986	Elmer Anderson	**1988**	E. Ben Davis
	Art Finney		Samuel Gee
	Richard "Night Train" Lane		Althea Gibson
	Joe Louis		Marshall Williams
1987	Thelma Cowans	**1989**	LaFayette Allen-Bowling
	Leroy Dues		Brewster Old Timers (1920-Present)
	Norman "Turkey" Steams		Samuel Lee Washington
	Sugar Ray Robinson		Muhammad Ali - Boxing
	John L. Klin		Wilma Randolph - Track
			Ron Teasley - Coach

Mississippi

Jackson

Smith Robertson Black Cultural Center
528 Bloom Street
Jackson, Mississippi 39207
(601) 960-1457

"A race without a History is like a ship without a rudder."
Located in the heart of Jackson's historic Black community, the Smith Robertson Museum is named in honor of a Black community leader who served Jackson as an Alderman from 1893-1899. Smith Robertson was born a slave in Fayette, Alabama, in 1840. He moved to Meridian, Mississippi, in 1869 to work as a barber with his brother. He moved to Jackson in 1874, where he became an outstanding citizen devoting himself to the education of Black youth. At a time when popular support for Black education in Mississippi was almost nonexistent, Mr. Robertson's urging influenced the city fathers to establish this school. In 1897, he was appointed a trustee.

The museum building occupies the site of Jackson's first public school building for Blacks. The original building, erected in 1894, burned in 1909 and was rebuilt that same year. An addition to the building in 1928 is an early, but sophisticated, example of Art Deco design in Mississippi. The school closed in June 1970, after 76 years of service. Through the efforts of interested citizens, the City of Jackson, and the Mississippi Department of Archives and History, the school building was renovated for use as a museum in 1984.

The Smith Robertson Museum interprets the life, history, and culture of Black Mississippians. Its exhibits feature life in the Farish Street Historic District and in Mississippi, the contributions of Blacks to education, business and politics, and the art of Black Mississippi folk artists and craftsmen. The museum's annual events include Black History Month Celebration, Freedom Festival, Anniversary Celebration, and Festival of Christmas Trees.

Missouri

St. Louis

Vaughn Cultural Center
5205 North Grand
Room 205
St. Louis, Missouri 63103
(314) 535-9227

The center was established in 1977 through a gift from Mrs. Ermalene Vaughn in honor of her husband, St. Louis physician.

The Vaughn Cultural Center strives to increase the awareness and understanding of Afro-American history and culture. The Center sponsors cultural events and activities year-round in the St. Louis metropolitan area. It is astonishing that such a relatively neophyte cultural center could produce such quality in varied programming. In its brief history, the center has: researched and produced two exhibitions, coordinated dozens of shows by local artists, presented speakers such as Julian Bond, Maya Angelou and Ossie Davis and Ruby Dee, produced a 30-minute film on the elderly and worked in conjunction with most of St. Louis major cultural institutions. The Center sponsors cultural events and activities year-round in the St. Louis metropolitan area. Programs include lectures, demonstrations; slide presentations, exhibits, performances and educational classes by local and national artists.

The Vaughn Cultural Center provides opportunities for all ages to learn about different cultures. The center sponsors workshops, classes, study groups, lectures and film series on African, Afro-American, Latin-American and Caribbean History, arts and cultures. The center houses an extensive library of books on Black History, culture and art.

Kansas City

Bruce R. Watkins
Cultural Heritage Center
3700 Blue Parkway
Kansas City, Missouri 64130
(816) 923-6226

Today and tomorrow began with yesterday's vision. The early Black pioneers envisioned Kansas City as a city of equality and greatness through hard work. Those dreams of the Black pioneers are now the responsibility of our community. The Bruce R. Watkins Foundation, Inc. and the Spirit of Freedom Fountain, Inc. in cooperation with the Kansas City, Missouri Department of Parks and Recreation began in 1981 to work together to bring the dreams of the late Bruce R. Watkins to fruition. It was Watkins who envisioned a facility that would pay tribute to those Black pioneers who had made significant contributions to the development of Kansas City.

Dreams can become reality. The Spirit of Freedom Fountain, with sculpture created by internationally known artist Richard Hunt, stands as a memorial to Watkins' dreams. Since the 1981 dedication of the Fountain, a variety of activities have been held to keep this dream alive.

The mission of the Bruce R. Watkins Interpretive Center is to actively research, discover, interpret, produce, collect, preserve and exhibit the history of the Kansas City area Black community. Through permanent and changing exhibitions, programs, activities, and educational outreach addressing all aspects of historic and contemporary Black life and culture in Kansas City, The Bruce R. Watkins Interpretive Center seeks to stimulate community involvement and awareness, develop museum scholarship and act as a springboard to assure links between the past, present and future.

With its galleries, library, research and educational facilities, and theater, The Bruce R. Watkins Interpretive Center will examine and house relevant documents and artifacts, and seeks to inspire the excitement of contemporary investigation, involvement and creativity invaluable to the community.

Kansas City

Negro Leagues Baseball Museum Inc.
1601 East 18th Street
Suite 260
Kansas City, Missouri 64108
(816) 221-1920

The museum was created to insure that the rich past of Black baseball and its profound affect on American society would not be lost. More than 2,600 players competed in the various Negro Baseball Leagues. Today only about 150 are still alive. Their stories and accomplishments chronicle a fascinating chapter in American history.

Baseball fans know the color line in organized baseball was broken in 1945 when Branch Rickey signed Jackie Robinson for the Brooklyn Dodgers organization. Few, however, have any appreciation of the baseball culture, which produced Jackie Robinson. Baseball behind the color barrier provided almost everything, and in some cases, more than was offered by Major League Baseball. There were World Series, All-Star games, bitter rivalries, packed stadiums, great tales of courage and most of all, talented players.

Research Center
The Research Center will house a custom designed database for searching the play by play of Negro League games.

Proposed Exhibit Rooms
Adults and children alike will enjoy creative exhibit areas. Displays of rare baseball memorabilia will come alive with excitement.
- World Series Room
- East-West All-Star Room
- Jackie Robinson Room
- Eastern Colored Room
- Rube Foster Room

Interpretive Exhibits
There will be visitor - activated displays and video presentations throughout the Museum.

NEW JERSEY

Jersey City

Afro-American Historical and Cultural Museum
1841 John F. Kennedy Boulevard
Jersey City, New Jersey 07305
(201) 547-5262

The Afro-American Historical and Cultural Society Museum began in October 1977 as an idea of Captain Thomas Taylor, President of the Jersey City branch of the N.A.A.C.P. Captain Taylor, at the time saw a need in the Jersey City Community to develop the historic and cultural understanding of the local residents. Toward this end he contacted Theodore Brunson, a local lay historian in the field of Afro-American history; Mrs. Nora Fant, a long time and active resident of Jersey City; and Mrs. Virginia Dunnaway, a community worker and teacher. Together they formed the Historical and Cultural Committee setting as its purpose the collection preservation and exhibition of Afro-American History: with particular emphasis of the city and county. From the beginning the committee decided that each year they would present programs and exhibitions on their discoveries.

Recently, the Afro-American Historical and Cultural Society Museum obtained a permanent location on the second floor of the Greenville Public Library. The trustees of the Jersey City Public Library granted the space and it gives rise to great optimism for the future as an incorporated entity with a permanent location.

NEW YORK

Brooklyn

Simmons Collection
African Arts Museum
1063 Fulton Street
Brooklyn, New York 11238
(718) 230-0933

The Simmons Collection African-Arts Museum is a non-funded, private Museum. The Museum has held tribal art exhibitions since 1976, but was not officially opened until 1983. The African Arts exhibited at the museum is of excellent quality and provides a rare opportunity in the New York community for learning about traditional African Arts and their relation to the African societies that created them.

Within the collection are traditional and contemporary arts, consisting of a wide range of masks and statuary, musical instruments, jewelry, paintings, tapestries, etc. The museum's treasures have been acquired over the past 17 years and are the private collection of Standfield Simmons, the museum's founder, director and curator. While organizing the Simmons Collection, Mr. Simmons has traveled to 27 different countries on the African Continent since 1970, areas covering most of the territories comprising west, central and east Africa.

The "Simmons Collection African Arts Museum" is a cultural center and educational institution dedicated to the:

- Preservation of African Arts and Cultures
- Cultivation of an appreciation for the artistic merits and underlying cultural values expressed in African sculptures
- Exploration of Africa's spiritually and socially cohesive societies, within their proper cultural context through an understanding of the functions, purposes, and symbolic language of traditional tribal art forms.
African contributions to the cultural history of mankind reach back to the beginning of human history.

New York

Hatch - Billops Collection
491 Broadway 7th Floor
New York, New York 10012
(212) 966-3231

The Hatch-Billops Collection is a research library founded in 1975 for three major purposes: (1) to collect and preserve primary and secondary resource materials in the Black Cultural Arts, (2) to provide tools and access to these materials for artists and scholars, as well as the general public; and (3) to develop programs in the arts which use the resources of the Collection.

Slide Collection: Approximately 10,000 35 mm color slides of artists, their work and exhibitions 1973 to present.

Oral History Tapes: 950 taped interviews with artists of all disciplines, 1970 to present. A series of interviews with an artist concerning the little known artists and teachers who inspired and instructed him or her.

In the past, the series has included Dizzy Gillespie, Ray Eldridge, Hazel Bryant, Talley Beatty, Amiri Baraka, Charlie Chin, John A. William, Fay Chiang, Bruce Nugent, Patti Bown, George Takei, Micki Grant, Krishma Reddy, Jimmy Owens, and many others.

Exhibition Catalogs: Approximately 1300 references to group and one person shows from 1930's to present.

There are displays of art work and artist memorabilia, sometimes in conjunction with special programs. For example, the manuscripts, letters, photos, programs, books of Owen Dodson were exhibited during the "Remembering Owen Dodson" memorial program where four specialists were invited to speak on Dodson's art and influences. The Owen and Edith Dodson Memorial Collection.

Established in 1984 in memory of the poet, playwright, and Howard University drama professor and his sister, Edith, this collection consists of manuscripts, published and unpublished, theatre programs, play scripts, poems, photographs, correspondence, newspaper reviews, and tape recording covering the periods from the 1930's to the time of their deaths in 1983. This unique collection will be cataloged and made accessible in 1987.

Theatre Program: 575 theatre program from New York City as well as other production around the nation and abroad, from 1890's to present.

Plays Published and Unpublished: Approximately 300 plays by Black American writers from 1858 to present.

Rosters: Approximately 450 including theatre, dance, poetry, exhibitions and others, from 1920's to present.

Vertical Files: Approximately 3000 folders of clippings, letter announcements, brochures, etc. on dance, theatre, art, film, literature, and T.V.

Photographs: Approximately 1000 black and white photos of artists, dancers, exhibitions, etc. Many are copies of scrapbook photos dating from 1890's to the present.

Books: Approximately 3500 books on the cultural arts, including histories, literature, poetry, art, dance, film, fascism, theatre, etc. The Black American Art and Theatre sections are as complete as any in the world, and include foreign publications.

Periodicals: Approximately, 1400 issues dating from 1890's to the present. Most are all or in part devoted to one or several aspects of the cultural arts.

Corona

>Louis Armstrong House
>Queens College Cuny
>34-56 107 Street Queens
>Corona, New York 11368
>(718) 478-8274
>(718) 478-8297

Louis Armstrong lived in a house on 107th Street, Corona Queens, from 1943 until his death in 1971. His wife Lucille, who lived there until she passed away in 1983, willed the house to the City of New York. The City in turn placed Queens College in charge of operating the Louis Armstrong House and Archive.

Louis Armstrong was born in a poor section of New Orleans on July 4, 1900. At the age of 13, following a street incident, Louis was sent to the Colored Waifs Home. During his three years there, he learned to play the coronet without musical training. In the late 1920s when he was already a force in jazz music, Armstrong switched from coronet to trumpet in order to reach a larger audience. By 1929, he had moved to New York and was becoming internationally known.

Appearing in several Hollywood movies during the 1930s increased Satchmo's following. He rose to a peak of popularity as a singer/personality with songs such as "Mack the Knife" (1955) and "Hello Dolly" (1964), the latter song knocking the Beatles from their number one place on the record charts.

The Archive contains hundreds of recordings, notes, and personal items that belonged to the legendary jazz trumpeter. But what the public seems to enjoy most are the photographs that capture the life and times of Satchmo.

A plague presented by the National Park Services, U.S. Department of the Interior, officially recognizes that the Louis Armstrong House is a national historic landmark.

New York

        The Black Fashion Museum
        157 West 126th Street
        New York, New York 10027
        (212) 666-1320

This museum is a cultural institution, which serves as a repository for garments designed and/or executed by black people as far back as possible. The museum officially opened on October 21, 1979. It is located at 155 West 126th Street next door to Harlem Institute of Fashion.

The story of the museum has been published in a book, <u>Blacks in the History of Fashion</u>, which is in essence the history of the contributions of Black people in the fashion industry---the first book of its kind.

The uniqueness of the museum, as well as its strength, lies in its permanent collection. The Black Fashion Museum "contains the most outstanding collection of the history of Black design and fashion information and memorabilia to be found anywhere in America." (I Love New York Harlem Travel Guide). It's the inaugural gown of Mary Todd Lincoln made by Elizabeth Keckley; two gowns designed by the late Ann Lowe Designer of the wedding gown of Jacqueline Kennedy Onassis when she married Senator John Fitzgerald Kennedy; a dress made by Rosa Parks, "The Mother of the Civil Rights Movement," and costumes from Broadway plays "The Wiz," "Eubie." and "Bubbling Brown Sugar."

The Black Fashion Museum is recognized as a major repository of rare items conceived in Black minds and designed and sewn by Black hands.

New York

        Schomburg Center For Research In Black Culture
        (The New York Public Library)
        515 Lenox Avenue
        New York, New York 10037-1801
        (212) 862-4000

Arthur A. Schomburg was born in San Juan, Puerto Rico on January 24, 1874. He spent much of his life working to disapprove a teacher's remark that "the Negro had no history." Having been educated mainly in Puerto Rico, he left New York in 1891, was soon teaching in the Central Evening High School. In 1896 Schomburg joined the Bankers Trust Company where he worked for over twenty years, all the time continuing his search for his lost heritage.

From 1904 he wrote hundreds of articles, speeches and letters to the editor relating to the Black experience. In 1915, he helped found the Negro Society for Historical Research and seven years later was elected President of the American Negro Academy. By this time he had become well known among rare book dealers everywhere. John Edward Bruce, scholar and activist W.E. B. DuBois, and Countee Cullen were among the friends who dropped by to peruse his growing collection of Black cultural treasures. When it came to the New York Public Library in 1926, it was one of the most important such private collections in the world; he had gathered over 5,000 volumes, 3,000 manuscripts, 2,000 etchings and portraits, and several thousand pamphlets.

After serving as Curator of Fisk University Library's New Negro Collection, Mr. Schomburg returned to New York in 1932 to head The New York Public Library's Division containing his collection. His work of fostering that collection continued until his death at 64 on June 10, 1938.

Arthur Alfonso Schomburg's legacy to future generations is the irreplaceable treasures in the Schomburg Center for Research in Black Culture.

NORTH CAROLINA

Sedalia

Charlotte Hawkins Brown Historical Foundation Inc.
Drawer G
Sedalia, North Carolina 27342
(919) 449-6515

When eighteen year old Charlotte Eugenia Hawkins returned to her native North Carolina in 1901 to teach rural Black children in what is now Sedalia, ten miles east of Greensboro, nobody even knew she was coming.

Certainly, they didn't know she'd be making history. Only one year after her arrival, the American Missionary Association School she was teaching in closed. Undaunted, and already committed to the education of these academically deprived children of North Carolina's Piedmont, Miss Hawkins journeyed back to New England.

She stayed only one summer, in which she raised enough money from friends, associates and New England philanthropists to return to her home state and begin her own school. In 1902, Miss Hawkins founded the Alice Freeman Palmer, a New England educator, and the first woman President of Wellesley, College. Dr. Palmer was one of Charlotte Hawkins' first and most influential patrons, and introduced the young educator to New England philanthropists such as Miss Helen F. Kimball and Mrs. Osbourn W. Bright. Later, Boston financier Mr. Galen Stone and Dr. Charles Eliot, President of Harvard, also became important benefactors to the school.

For over fifty years, Dr. Charlotte Hawkins Brown presided over Palmer, which became one of the nation's most distinguished Black preparatory schools, with over one thousand students from across the nation confirming Dr. Brown's vision of an education which would enable Black children to become "educationally efficient, religiously sincere, and culturally secure."

Today, the legacy of one of America's most gifted educators and humanitarians, Dr. Charlotte Hawkins Brown lives on. The journey continues, with the State of North Carolina's preservation of a state historic site honoring Dr. Brown, and the Charlotte Hawkins Brown Historical Foundation's plans for a progressive, prolific future promoting North Carolina's proud heritage of Black history.

The Charlotte Hawkins Brown Historical Foundation, Inc. is a private, non-profit organization incorporated in September 1983 to support and assist the State of North Carolina in establishing the first Black historic site in North Carolina.

The Foundation works closely with the North Carolina Department of Cultural Resources, Division of Archives and History, Historic Sites Section, and other interested organizations in the preservation and appreciation of North Carolina African-American history. Its offices are located just next door to Dr. Brown's home, Canary Cottage, in Sedalia, North Carolina, on the former campus of the Palmer Memorial Institute, which in November, 1987 was designated a State Historic Site. Carrie M. Stone Teacher's Cottage, home of the foundation, also houses a state visitor's center and numerous other exhibits honoring Dr. Brown and Palmer Memorial Institute.

Less than five years ago, the 350 acre former Palmer campus, home of one of this nation's premiere Black preparatory schools for almost 70 years, lay dormant and deteriorating abandoned, and in imminent danger of being lost forever to the past.

Thanks to the collaborative efforts to the State of North Carolina, the Charlotte Hawkins Brown Historical Foundation, Inc. numerous friends, associates and Palmer alumni, North Carolina's first historic site honoring an African-American, and a woman now-features a museum, a visitor's reception center, and a gift shop commemorating Dr. Brown and Palmer Memorial Institute in the recently renovated Carrie M. Stone Teacher's Cottage.

Charlotte

Afro-American Culture Center
401 North Myers Street
Charlotte, North Carolina 28202
(704) 374-1565

The Center was founded in 1974 to promote, present and preserve the culture of African-Americans through arts and cultural programming. This project is made possible by a grant from the North Carolina Humanities Council, a foundation supported by federal tax funds and private gifts, whose purpose is to encourage and assist public education activities in the humanities for adults.

The realization of the Afro-American Cultural and Service Center is the direct result of the vision and intense commitment of its founders, Dr. Mary Harper and Dr. Bertha Maxwell - Roddy, and a united effort of the Charlotte community to develop among all citizens an increased awareness, understanding and appreciation of Afro-American culture and history.

Asheville

YMI Cultural Center, Inc.
Market and Eagle Streets
P.O. Box 7301
Asheville, N.C. 28807
(704) 252-4614

The YMI Cultural Center is committed to cultural and economic development of minorities in Western North Carolina. Planning for programs began in 1981 and activities were under way in 1983.

- Local Black History
- Ethnic Cultural Arts
- Minority Economic Development
- Neighborhood Redevelopment
- New Ventures

The economic development component materialized when YMICC reclaimed the YMI building from urban blight in 1980. The YMI building held a tradition of service to the Black community of Western North Carolina for eighty years, as it has housed in earlier years: the Negro branch of the Public Library; the Negro branch of the YMCA; a literacy society; the first kindergarten for Black children; an auditorium which was utilized by the Black Elementary City Schools; a commitment to preserve the building lead to the initial incorporation of the YMICC, as it had been added to the National Register of Historic Places in 1970.

The art gallery and cultural arts component opened seeking an understanding and appreciation of Black art forms and Black culture. This component also seeks to develop quality Black drama, music and visual arts organizations locally.

Ohio

Cleveland

Karamu House, Inc.
2355 East 89th Street
Cleveland, Ohio 44106-9990
(216) 795-7077

Karamu House opened as a settlement house in 1915, serving the areas referred to as the "roaring third," a rectangle from East 14th Street to East 55th Street between Carnegie and Woodland Avenues.

Originally known as the "Playhouse Settlement" of the Neighborhood Association and located in a small framed house at East 38th and Central Avenue, the organization became a center of the community or "Karamu," a Swahili word meaning "central place of group activity."

From its inception, the performing and visual arts constituted an important part of the total Karamu program. The Jellifies used the arts as a human relations tool, bringing people of diverse cultural and racial backgrounds together for mutual understanding.

Karamu House is a metropolitan center for the arts charged with serving people of all ages and races while adhering to and promoting high standards of excellence in the provision of education and training in the performing, visual and cultural arts. Karamu also accepts the unique responsibility of providing avenues and develop their skills and talents.

Karamu houses two theatres: a 223-seat Proscenium Theatre and an Arena Theatre, which seats 110-120. The performing arts season is designed to offer eight (8) to eleven (11) productions, which include musicals, dramas and new works. Productions run four to six weeks Thursday through Sunday.

Karamu takes special pride in its two art galleries, offering a fine array of works created by emerging and underexposed artists. Karamu's Proscenium Gallery has been described as "one of the finer small exhibit spaces in the city," and is recognized for its presentation of first class works. Another integral part of the art department is the Bokari Gift Shop. The Bokari, meaning "market place," in Swahili, features a fine display of ceramic gift items created by Karamu art students past and present, and includes prints, jewelry, tee-shirts and other unique items designed by area artists.

Cleveland

Black History Archives
The Western Reserve
Historical Society Library
10825 East Boulevard
Cleveland, Ohio 44106
(216) 721-5722

The Western Reserve Historical Society established the Black History Archives in 1970 to collect the papers of individuals and the records of organizations that have been active in the Greater Cleveland area. Specifically, the archives seek correspondence, record books, newspaper, pamphlets and books, scrapbooks, and photographs. These materials are arranged, cataloged, and housed in the Society's modern library building where they are made available for research, exhibitions, and publications.

This project was established in 1970 through a two-year grant from the Cleveland Foundation; thereafter it was continued largely through the Society's own operating funds. Over the twenty years the project staff sought out and acquired over one hundred major collections of photographs and manuscripts relating to the Black experience in Cleveland. Among these were the 40,000 negatives of local Black photographer Allen E. Cole, the records of the local branches of the N.A.A.C.P. and Urban

League, the records of the papers of notable black community figures such as Thomas Fleming, Carol Stokes, and Russell Davis.

As these collections have been cataloged and made available for research, they have served as the basis for every major investigation of the local black experience. While the scholarly impact of the BHAP has been substantial, its presence in the local community has been of even greater consequence. The Black History Archivist regularly delivered lectures to school classes, seminars, and community organizations on the subject of local Black history.

Cleveland

African-American Cultural
And Historical Society Museum
1765 Crawford Road
Cleveland, Ohio 44106
(216) 791-1700

Brief History

The African-American Museum (formerly the Afro-American Cultural and Historical Society Museum) is located at in Cleveland, Ohio in the former Treasure House Branch of the Cleveland Public Library.

The museum was founded in 1953 by Icabod Flewellen and incorporated in December of 1960. It has been at its current location since fall 1984. The move to this location was the result of a cooperative effort on the part of the City of Cleveland, the Cleveland Public Library and the museum supporters.

Purpose of the museum is to:

- Collect, house, preserve, research, share and publicly display information and artifacts that tell the story of the magnitude of the great and noble contributions of the people of African descent and how these contributions were at the center of human progress from the foundation of the world;
- Encourage the support of African and African American creativity and enterprise.
- Encourage the display of cultural items in homes, schools, churches, and businesses; and
- Make available a broad range of esteem building materials including books, art, lectures, forums and cultural events.

Dayton

Dunbar House
219 Paul Lawrence Dunbar Avenue
Dayton, Ohio 45407
(937) 224-7061

Paul Laurence Dunbar was born in 1872 and grew up in poverty. His mother, Matilda took in washing to help keep food on the table while Paul and his two half-brothers took odd jobs to supplement her income. What Matilda could not provide in material wealth, she provided in inspiration to her youngest son. She gave Paul a rich treasure of stories from her past, a love of song, and poetry, much love and encouragement and the desire to achieve.

The Dunbar House is a beautiful nine room structure. Paul Laurence purchased this house upon returning from Washington in 1903. Having died in 1906, the poet lived here just three years however his mother Mrs. Matilda Dunbar remained here until her death in 1934. Mrs. Dunbar left the house to her son, Robert Murphy who resided in Chicago. After a few years, the house was declared a state monument.

The home Paul lived and worked in with his mother Matilda became a state memorial after her death in 1934. The Ohio Historical Society acquired the home after the State of Ohio bought the house from Matilda's estate. Today, the house is devoted to the exhibition and care of artifacts belonging to and the study of the life of Paul Laurence Dunbar. It has recently undergone a historical restoration and renovation returning it to turn-of-the century splendor and elegance. Among the objects on view are the desk and typewriter. Dunbar used to compose much of his poetry; the ceremonial sword presented to him by President Theodore Roosevelt, and the bicycle the Wright Brothers gave to Dunbar as a token of their friendship.

> *We wear the mask*
> *We wear the mask that grins and lies,*
> *It hides our cheeks and shades our eyes, -*
> *This debt we pay to human guile;*
> *With torn and bleeding hearts we smile,*
> *And mouth with myriad subtleties.*
> *Why should the world be over wise?*
> *In counting all our tears and signs?*
> *Nay let them only see us, while*
> *We wear the mask.*

Findlay

> Black Studies & Library Association
> of Findlay and Hancock County
> 839 Liberty Street
> Findlay, Ohio 45840
> (419) 423-4954

Nina G. Parker a Findlay resident established the Black history library with a sincere concern regarding the limited area information on African and African-American history. With the support of family and friends the idea for a library was realized in 1982. The library was originally housed in Mason Chapel African Methodist Episcopal Church under the ministry of Rev. Dolphus L. Smith and supervision of the Church Stewardess Board.

The library is now independently operated and managed by the Black Studies & Library Association of Findlay and Hancock County (B.S.L.A.), which is a non-profit educational organization, dedicated to enhancing public awareness of the contributions, history, and culture of Black people. In July of 1987, a building was acquired to separately house and more adequately meet the needs and concerns of library patrons.

Services
- Over 400 books with information and material suitable for age levels ranging from pre-school to adult.
- A variety of periodicals and magazines
- Audio-Visual materials including video cassette selections
- A showcase display of authentic African, African-American, Haitian, and Caribbean art and artifacts
- An assortment of pictures and poster (available for loan) depicting the contributions and history of Black people
- Story-Time for children to be featured in the Fall

- Speakers, slide shows, and other out-reach program
- Cultural arts and gifts for sale

Wilberforce

National Afro-American Museum
and Cultural Center
P.O. Box 578
Wilberforce, Ohio 45384
(513) 376-4944
1-800-BLK-HIST

The National Afro-American Museum and Cultural Center was originally organized as a joint project of the State of Ohio and the federal government. Located on the historic 88 acre site of the Old Wilberforce University campus, the first phase of this state-of-the-art complex includes the newly constructed 35,000 square foot museum and the renovated Carnegie Library.

- 55,000 square feet exhibition space
- Center for Historical Research-Library & Manuscript Collections
- Art Gallery
- Classrooms
- Conference Center
- Conservation Laboratories
- Exhibit Fabrication Workshops
- 20,000 square feet of collection storage space
- Theater and Amphitheater
- Cafeteria and picnic areas

Discover the era of the "Fifties" - a dramatic period of change in American society. Learn of the diversity and complexity of the African-American experience at a time when the nation was challenged to fulfill its promise of justice and equality for all.

PENNSYLVANIA

Philadelphia

Afro-American Historical and Cultural Museum
7th & Arch Streets
Philadelphia, Pennsylvania 19106-1557
(215) 574-0380

The museum was the first specifically built by a major city in the United States to house and interpret collections of African-American culture. The museum is an actively collecting institution whose holdings include, historical artifacts, photographs, furnishings, fine arts, documents as well as books on African-American history and culture and African art.

The continued development of the museum's collections is a high priority, and this commitment has resulted in some extraordinary donations such as the collection of Jack Franklin, a freelance photographer whose collection includes 300,000 negatives and photographs which document nearly 40 years of Black cultural, social and political life.

Other donations include: a collection of photographs, memoirs, drawings and paintings of Anne Russell Jones, the first African-American graduate from the Moore College of Art; and the Lloyd

Thompson, William Cash collection of documents, photographs and memorabilia which chronicles the Hilldale Baseball Club of Darby, Pennsylvania, one of the Negro League teams, from 1910 to the 1950s.

The museum's exhibits are central elements of holistic interpretive programs. Exhibitions put objects and images into historical or cultural context; tours, lectures, gallery talks, discovery activities, films and symposia develop specific interpretive themes; performances complement the exhibits; and openings and other special events are used to highlight major objects, images and ideas.

Pennsylvania

Philadelphia

Philadelphia Doll Museum
7257 North 18th Street
Philadelphia, Pennsylvania 19126
(215) 924-3121

Ms. Whiteman is the founder of the Philadelphia Doll Museum and the organizer of the First Annual Black Doll Show and Sale on the east coast.
Barbara A. Whiteman is an enthusiastic Black doll collector whose unique collection developed from a love of studying Black history and culture. She believes the searching, researching, and publication of Black dolls are an essential part of Black history. Ms. Whiteman has traveled across the nation lecturing on the "History of Black Dolls." The lecture offers the history and identification of 30 or more special Black dolls and Black doll collecting. Included also is the doll artist's portrayal of Black dolls.

Dark Images is an educational presentation of Black history and the evolution of Black dolls. More than play objects or toys, these Black dolls symbolize the struggle for freedom and human dignity. Each doll has a message of truth and strength that is important to the psychological and sociological development of Black people. Collectively, they present visual images of how Black people were perceived throughout world history. Dark Images has been presented to many organizations, schools and churches.

The collection shows Black dolls from the late 1800s through the 1980s such as authentic African dressed dolls, German and French Black bisque dolls, Black American Folk dolls, collectibles, composition and hard plastic, and modern vinyl. There are personality dolls featuring advertising and T.V. celebrities and famous people.

Rhode Island

Providence

Rhode Island Black Heritage Society
1 Hilton Street
Providence, Rhode Island 02905
(401) 751-3490

The Rhode Island Black Heritage Society founded in 1975, is the only Black historical society in the state of Rhode Island. It's primary goal is to research, document, exhibit, and interpret the history of Blacks in Rhode Island. For the first three years of it's existence, the Society was aided by and housed in the Rhode Island Historical Society. The joint years not only helped the (RIBHS) to establish itself financially and programmatically, but also cemented a working relationship with the Rhode Island Historical Society which continues to the present. In 1979, the Society moved into it's new facilities as part of the new Opportunities Industrial Center in Providence. In this rented space the Society enlarged it's available area for storage, exhibits, and meetings as well as gaining access to auditorium, and additional programming facilities.

As an organization committed to documenting and bringing into the public sphere the history of the Afro-American presence in Rhode Island, the Society has established an impressive record of support for educational projects which span a broad range.

The Society's purpose is to reconstruct Black history and to find and preserve the cultural material, wherever possible, that tells that history. Over the years, the Society has worked diligently to improve the quality of its research, in addition to developing the means to interpret and impart that knowledge to the general community, by means of exhibits, lectures and other programs.

The Society maintains an ongoing exhibition program over the past decade serving as an institutional anchor for oral history, folklore, and musicology projects. In addition to the exhibits, programs and lectures the (RIBHS) has a very active outreach program.

SOUTH CAROLINA

Columbia

>Mann-Simons Cottage
>Museum of African-American Culture
>1403 Richland Street
>Columbia, South Carolina 29201
>(803) 252-1450

Few details of Celia Mann's life as a free Black woman of Columbia are actually known. However, family and community tradition indicate that she had been born and reared in slavery in Charleston and that she purchased her freedom and walked to Columbia in the early nineteenth century. Born in 1799 Celia Mann had acquired over $2,000 in real estate before her death in 1867. An uneducated, propertied midwife with four daughters, she left a legacy of achievement to her heirs. Celia's oldest daughter, Agnes Jackson Simons, a baker and laundress, inherited the Cottage upon her mother's death.

According to family, tradition, Agnes was married to a local musician named Bill Simons. She lived most of her life in the Cottage, which after her death became the property of her son, Charles Simons.

The Richland County Historic Preservation Commission and the Center led the movement of preserve and restore the Cottage for Black History, Art and Folklore. The Cottage, dated 1850, was restored to its 1880 appearance in 1977. Listed on the National's Register of Historic Places, it serves as a museum devoted to the preservation and presentation of African-American culture.

The house contains the history of one family of Black citizens, who represent the picture of how free Blacks of Columbia's antebellum period lived and worked. Six percent of the city's population in 1850 was made up of free Blacks.

Orangeburg

>I.P. Stanback Museum and Planetarium
>South Carolina State College
>Orangeburg, South Carolina 29117
>Founded 1970's
>(803)536-7174

The idea for a museum and planetarium on the South Carolina State College campus dates back to the early 1970s. The museum began as the Whittaker Gallery in the basement of the College library. The building bears the name of the first Black chairman of the College's Board of Trustees, who served on the Board from 1966-1982.

The building includes a museum with one of the largest exhibit areas in the state. A forty-foot dome planetarium, the largest in the state, seats eighty-two people, and is located across the lobby from the museum. The facility is uniquely adaptable to many different types of presentations. The building is accessible to the handicapped.

The Planetarium

- Ft. Domed Projection Ceiling
- Theater - Style Seats
- Viewlex Series IIB Planetarium Projector
- Multi-Program Selective Effects System
- Sky Laboratory Sessions For College Astronomy Classes
- Graded Programs in Basic Astronomy for Elementary and Secondary School Classes

The Museum

From the time of its first acquisition, the museum has been dedicated to forming a collection of high quality art. The collection includes African artifacts and gemstones, photographs, prints, paintings and sculpture by African-American artists, and American art.

Charleston

>Avery Institute Research Center
>for Afro-American History and Culture
>P.O. Box 2262
>Charleston, South Carolina 29403
>(803) 792-5742

The course of Afro-American history has flowed deeply and dramatically over that portion of the Atlantic Coastal plain and the neighboring island, which lie between Charleston and the St. John's River in northern Florida. Known to residents as "the low country," the region displays a microcosm of the social forces that have shaped the historical experiences of Black Americans in the United States.

After 1720, the population of the South Carolina low country was a Black majority drawn from Africa and the Caribbean. Their labor as slaves on lowland indigo, rice, and long-staple cotton estates become the basis of plantation wealth, while black artisans in Charleston fashioned much of the wood, iron, and brick work of the town's famous houses and public buildings. During the Civil War, Black Carolinians joined northern teachers and plantation agents to sow, in the seed bed of succession, experiments in free labor and public education that became a rehearsal for reconstruction in the post-war South. In the aftermath of war and slavery, the hopes of ex-slaves to own land came closest to full realization along the Carolina coast, while the Black political leadership of South Carolina may have been influential than that of any other southern state. After 1880, black religious, business, fraternal, and civic organizations launched a struggle for equality whose legacy since 1940 has been enriched by a host of educational, political, labor, and civic groups.

The purpose of the Avery Research Center is to preserve and make public the history and cultural heritage of the Low country African-American community. The center is a cooperative project of the College of Charleston and the Avery Institute of Afro-American History and Culture, a local community-based Black-American historical society. When it is fully-established, the research center will include an archive and museum located on the site of the former Avery Normal Institute, the Charleston College - preparatory and normal school that trained Black teachers for nearly 100 years, beginning in 1865.

The College, The Avery Institute and the Charleston community share responsibility in the governance of the research center through representation on the Center's advisory board.

The purpose of the research center will be accomplished through: the establishment of a national archives, depository and registrar for information and material on Carolina Low-Country African-Americans, and the presentation of conferences, forums, exhibits, and other academic activities to be planned in cooperation with departments of the College of Charleston.

TENNESSEE

Chattanooga

Mary Walker Historical and Educational Foundation
3031 Wilcox Blvd.
Chattanooga, Tennessee 37411
(615) 622-3217

The Foundation was established in 1974. It's objectives are to motivate people to be productive citizens by providing eyes and hands on education.

Prior to the establishment of the Foundation, friends and well wishers, would celebrate Mary Walker's birthday by gathering at the Poss Homes High Rise for the elderly where she lived and now bares her name (Mary Walker Towers). The first big celebration was given her in 1966 when she received greetings from President Lyndon Johnson, Tennessee Governor Buford, Ellington and many other national, state, and local officials. Mary Walker was born May 6, 1848 in Union Springs, Alabama. May is officially proclaimed Mary Walker month in Chattanooga, Tennessee.

Mary Walker (1848-1969) - The fact that Mary Walker was a person who lived 121 years and seven months is not the most important aspect of her life, even when we view the conditions under which she lived. What she did, and the times in which she did it, is most important.

At a time when reading levels of children and adults were at their lowest point in America, Mary Walker had a desire for education that slavery and slums could not give. She enrolled in the Chattanooga Area Literacy Movement and learned to read and write at the age of 117.

The Health Education and Welfare Department proclaimed Mary Walker the oldest student in America. She had perfect memory and mental alertness and proved "you're never too old to learn."

The Foundation's aims and interests are concentrated in three main objectives.

(1) To create an atmosphere that is conducive to learning by generating a more positive attitude toward reading.

(2) To promote the study of history and Afro-American History.

(3) To keep abreast, discuss and make available information that is of educational, economical, religious and social value.

Housed within the Foundation is The Mary Walker Replica Slave Cabin Museum. The museum displays several artifacts associated with slavery as well as a variety of memoirs of the late Mary Walker. Thousands of people from school classrooms, church groups, and various organizations throughout Tennessee have toured the Museum and been inspired by the story of Mary Walker. The following are programs conducted in the museum:

- THE MARY WALKER TUTORING SCHOOL
- THE MARY WALKER HISTORY LIBRARY
- THE MARY READING MOVEMENT

Chattanooga

Chattanooga African-American Museum
730 Martin Luther King Blvd.
Chattanooga, Tennessee 37403
(615)267-1076

The Chattanooga African-American Heritage Museum and Research Center was incorporated and certified in 1983. The purpose of the organization is to provide a facility to house cultural and historical documents and artifacts portraying Black American's contributions to the growth of Chattanooga and the nation.
The specific objectives of the museum are;
- To discover and preserve the achievements of Black Americans, particularly those of Chattanoogans and to maintain a public center to research, record, and exhibit these achievements.
- To develop universal appreciation and interest in African-American heritage through community education; to develop meaningful approaches to - and materials for this awareness.
- To promote a better understanding of Black American culture.

The Chattanooga African-American Museum (CAAM) was born of a great need. At the time of its founding in 1983, sources in curriculum, historical references, creative works, and the media about the identity of Black Americans were limited and inaccessible to the average student or individual.

The museum has more than met the challenge of that need. Dedicated to the preservation and dissemination of local history and culture of Africans and Americans of African descent, the CAAM has, within the brief years of its existence, become a principal and valuable reservoir of primary and secondary source materials on almost every aspect of the social, cultural, religious, political and economic history of Black Americans.

The Chattanooga African-American Heritage Council was chartered in 1977, and established the Chattanooga American Heritage Museum and Research Center which is presently in the Central City Complex 730 Martin Luther King Blvd.

The community has helped the museum establish itself in the state and Chattanooga area as a beacon for community involvement and cultural awareness. There motto is, "History Has Been Made, It Is Up To Us To Preserve It!"

Henning

    Alex Haley State Historic Site and Museum
    200 S. Church and Haley Avenue
    Henning, Tennessee 38041
    (901) 738-2240

    Henning is the hometown of Pulitzer Prize winning author Alex Haley. The small West Tennessee town was the setting for much of his highly acclaimed novel, Roots. The book and the subsequent television, mini-series captured the hearts of people the world over.

    Haley's boyhood home is being restored to its 1919 appearance. Exhibits and memorabilia from both the book and movie will be displayed.

    Originally known as the Palmer House, the ten-room bungalow style home was constructed in 1919 by Will E. Palmer, the maternal grandfather of Alex Haley. Palmer was the first Black businessman of his kind in West Tennessee when he became proprietor of the local lumber mill.

    From 1921 to 1929, and for many summers afterwards, Alex Haley lived with his grandparents. Upon the front porch he heard oral accounts of family history from his grandmother, Cynthia Palmer, and aunts Liz, Plus, Viney, and Till, and cousin Georgia. They recounted stories of ancestor Kunta Kinte, the sixteen year old Mandigo warrior captured near his village of Juffure on the Kamby Balongo in West Africa and sold as a slave in Annapolis, Maryland. The women traced Kinte's lineage from his daughter, Kizzy, to her son, "Chicken George," the game cock trainer who won his freedom before the Emancipation Proclamation, who led the family from Alamance, North Carolina to the Western Tennessee settlement of Henning. These stories and the town of Henning inspired Haley to research and eventually write the Pulitzer Prize-winning novel, Roots and history of Henning, Tennessee.

    The Alex Haley House Museum is an excellent interpretation of rural small town life in the 1900's in West Tennessee. It is also the first African-American state historic site, and the only writer's home open to the public in Tennessee.

Knoxville

    Beck Cultural Exchange Center, Inc.
    1927 Dandridge Avenue
    Knoxville, Tennessee 37915
    (614) 524-8461

    Unique in its dedication to the best, the Beck named for James and Ethel Beck, prominent members of the Knoxville community and founders of the Ethel Beck Home for Orphans, provides opportunities for cultural exchange. These experiences preserve the achievements of Black's in Knoxville, the State of Tennessee and the nation.

    The William Henry Hastie Room which houses a permanent extensive collection of memorabilia of the first Black federal judge, the first Black governor of the Virgin Islands, and a native Knoxvillian.

    Beck Cultural Exchange Center is just minutes away from the birthplace of the State of Tennessee.

    It's easy to find one of Knoxville's "Hidden" Treasures.

TEXAS

Houston

Texas Southern University
University Library
Special Collections
3201 Wheeler Avenue
Houston, Texas 77004

- The Barbara Jordan Archives
- The Gallery of Traditional African Art
- The Heartman Collection

The establishment of the Barbara Jordan Archives at Texas Southern University provides for the Southwest a unique research facility of international significance. An extraordinary gift from one of the TSU's outstanding alumnae, this singular collection endows the University with a comprehensive collection of historical documents rarely found within the holdings of a traditional college library system.

The collection of Representative Jordan's papers, manuscripts and personal memorabilia span the period from 1967 through 1978. The early days of her career as an attorney, her activities in the Texas Senate and her outstanding contributions on Capitol Hill are all reflected in the collection. The archives permit a thorough analysis of the development of the career of one of this country's most distinguished congressional representative and provides for scholars of political science, history, and law the opportunity to examine in depth one of the most historically rich eras in the development of the United States. The Congressional collection includes Representative Jordan's remarks on the floor of the House, records from Judiciary Committee Hearings, bills introduced, legislative correspondence and selected speeches. Recorded transcripts and videotapes of interviews and speeches form a significant part of the collection

The archives serve as a source of inspiration and pride to students, and faculty of Texas Southern University and to members of the Houston community. The collection forms a magnificent complement to the other special collections housed at the University library.

The establishment of the Barbara Jordan Archives at Texas Southern University provides for the Southwest a unique research facility of international significance. An extraordinary gift from one of the most outstanding alumnae of the University, this singular collection endows the University with a comprehensive collection of historical documents rarely found within the holdings of a traditional college library system.

As early as 1971, the curator of the Heartman Collection of Negro Life and Culture at the Texas Southern University Library, Mrs. Dorothy Chapman, recognized the significance and importance of the political activity of Barbara C. Jordan to scholars of history and politics. Mrs. Chapman approached the then Senator from Harris County with the request that she deposit her papers with the University Library. Although Senator Jordan's response was that she had no papers suitable for deposit at that time, she agreed to keep the request in mind for an appropriate time in the future.

Subsequent to that initial inquiry, the Senator from Harris County became the Congresswoman from Texas serving in the Nation's Congress during one of the most turbulent eras in American political history. Her papers, now the files of the first Black in the Texas Senate and the first Black Texan in the U.S. Congress, represent a significant contribution to the documentation of American history.

When Representative Jordan opted to retire from Congress in 1978, the University again began negotiations to become the repository for the records of her career. On August 16, 1978, Representative Jordan, in a letter to the Vice President for University Relations, officially deposited her papers with the Texas Southern University Library.

The collection of traditional African art acquired by Texas Southern University over the past three decades brings an added dimension to the study of the humanities at the University. In view of the long evolutionary period, 10,000 years, of African traditional concepts in painting, pottery and sculpture, authorities recognize African traditional art as classical.

Fully catalogued, and installed in the gallery of the United Library, the collection has become a favorite area of interest. Composed of over 160 works of art from East, Central and West Africa, with selected works from the Pacific Islands and Meso-America, the collection is varied and vast enough in its scope to permit periodic changes in installation. Included in the collection are rare textiles, musical instruments, and ancestral figures. There are also fine examples of bronze casting, wood carving and weaving.

As a teaching collection, the works provided students with the unique experience of seeing, and under proper guidance, handling, objects, which were created for specific cultural functions. The collection serves at once to reflect the presence of world cultures at Texas Southern University and indicates in a concrete manner an appreciation for and understanding of the African Diaspora.

The Heartman Collection of Negro Life and Culture is a virile and vibrant testimony to the strength and spirit of Black people. The nucleus of the collection, 11,000 items, was purchased in 1948 from a German - born book dealer, Charles F. Heartman of Biloxi, Mississippi.

The collection contains books, pamphlets, lithographs, oil paintings, musical scores, almanacs, diaries, Texas slave narratives, scrapbooks, and other documents specifically pertaining to the growth and development of Black people in Texas, the United States and the world. The holdings of the Heartman Collection currently number more than 25,000 items and include the popular and contemporary along with the rare and historical.

The Heartman Collection is extremely significant. It has been called the largest and most comprehensive research collection on Blacks to be found in the southwest United States. The collection has value for the researcher and also for the student whose interest in Black life, history and culture is more general.

Texas

Austin

George Washington Carver Museum
Public Library
1165 Angelina Street
Austin, Texas 78702
(512) 472-4809

The George Washington Carver Museum has the distinction of being the first local Black history neighborhood museum in the state of Texas. Located on the perimeter of Kealing Park, the museum serves the needs of citizens of Austin through the collection and preservation of books, photographs, manuscripts, city/county reports, maps, and other informational material which document the history of Blacks on city, county, state, and national levels.

The museum is housed in a city owned - building, which was originally located at the corner of Ninth and Guadalupe Streets and served as the old Main Library. This frame structure was moved to East Austin in 1933. Its exterior was resurfaced in a brick veneer, and it reopened as the Austin Public Library's first branch.

The Carver Museum has continued to serve the needs of the public by presenting a variety of exhibitions related to Black history and culture. Exhibitions have included "George Washington Carver:

Cookstove Chemist," a display of photographs and artifacts documenting the life of Dr. Carver; " From the Grounds Up, a Look at an Historic Austin Community," a photographic exploration of East Austin; and "Martin Luther King, Jr. and the Civil Rights Movement," a traveling exhibit from the Texas Humanities Resource Center.

Austin

    Black Texan's Hall of Fame, Inc.
    920 E. 11th Street
    P.O. Box 15103
    Austin, Texas 78753
    (512) 472-5731
    (512) 837-1450

The Black Texan's Cultural Museum/Hall of Fame was organized April 25, 1987 at a state wide conference held on the campus of Huston-Tillotson College in Austin, Texas.

The Hall of Fame will provide Black Texans, young and old, with information of exemplary participation of individual Afro-Americans in important period of Texas history.

Blacks were as much a part of the daily life in Texas as the Mexicans, Americans or Europeans. Some were free but most were slaves. It was not until after the slaves obtained freedom in 1865 that they were able to make lasting contributions to history in Texas.

Researchers will note the significant contributions of Blacks throughout the history of Texas and their contributions will be preserved in the Black Texans Hall of Fame.

Dr. David A. Williams stated the dream, his ideas were approved and the Dream, became a reality. The objective is to establish a museum to house information about Afro-Americans in Texas.

Dallas

    Museum of African-American
    Life and Culture
    P.O. Box 41511
    Dallas, Texas 75241
    (214) 565-9026

This museum will be the only one of its kind in the Southwest. It will feature visual art and historic documents relating to Black life in Dallas, the Southwest, and the United States.

The African-American museum was founded in 1974 as part of Bishop College in the basement, and has supported itself as an independent agency since 1979.

The Heritage Center, focal point of this latest campaign, will serve as the library/archives and permanent history gallery of the museum.

The museum will be of ivory stone, dominated by a 60-foot gray dome. Its two stories and basement will house four galleries, a community room, classrooms, theater, and an arts and crafts area, along with the library/archive selections.

The new museum will be located near the site of the Hall of Negro Life erected for the 1936 Texas Centennial Exposition. It will be a magnificent new building, in the heart of Dallas, preserving the history, culture and art of Black Americans for future generations.

Houston

African-American Heritage Museum
2101 Crawford Suite 111A
Houston, Texas 77002
(713) 759-0044

The African American Heritage Museum of Houston was founded in 1988 in an effort to complete the cultural heritage of the Southwestern Region of the United States. The museum was established for the purpose of identifying, collecting, preserving, and exhibiting art objects and historical artifacts relevant to the African-American experience.

One of the ongoing goals is to establish a major museum to serve as both a center for exceptional exhibits as well as a repository to display the artistic and cultural history of people of color, the Black Indian and Blacks, particularly those of the Southwest.

This museum will provide for the general public of all ages an educational resource for the research and study of the artistic and cultural contributions of African-Americans.

The primary focus of the institution will be a museum that is "alive" and programs that will excite the imagination of children. The primary mediums to be employed are artifacts, art works, performing artists, audio, video, and slide presentations, hands on exhibits/seminars, and tours.

Lest We Not Forget...

"Look at Africa, the land from whence my father came three hundred years ago. We despise her today because we do not know her history. Three hundred years ago no Negroes were to be found in these United States of America on this North America continent, in the West Indies and South and Central America." *Marcus Garvey,* From *his Letters - 1920 - 1922*

VIRGINIA

Roanoke

Harrison Museum of African-American Culture
523 Harrison Avenue, N.W.
P.O. Box 194
Roanoke, Virginia 24002
(703) 345-4818

"...a haven for the arts and treasures of a strong and mighty race."

The Harrison Center came into being through the dreams of a few farsighted citizens, and the hard work and cooperation of Total Action Against Poverty (TAP), the City of Roanoke, Fralin & Waldron, and community leaders.

After six years of planning, the Harrison Heritage Center celebrated a gala opening in October, 1985. Harrison School is once again a hub of community life, with 28 apartments for the elderly on the upper floors, and a vibrant new center on the ground floor.

It is a testament to a tradition of caring commitment that is being continued as the Center evolves as a major cultural facility, creating linkages between the old and the new, the present and the future, black and white.

The Harrison Center is nothing like a cathedral. A trim brick building with crisp white accents located at Fifth Street and Harrison Avenue, it looks exactly like what it is: a turn-of-the-century public school house.

But not just any school house. Opened in 1917, the Harrison School became the only high school in Southwest, Virginia for Blacks; prior to its construction, blacks wanting more than an eighth-grade education had to travel to Petersburg.

Nor is the classic Georgian exterior to be taken for granted. By the late 1970s years of sitting vacant had left the building assaulted, battered and vandalized by the weather, street gangs and drifters. Demands from local residents that the eyesore is torn down were so frequent, recalls assistant city manager Earl Reynolds that a demolition plan was already on file and awaiting funds.

And then along came Hazel Thompson - as well as Cabell Brand, Bern Ewert, Horace Fralin, Jim Olin and a slew of other unlikely cathedral builders - to reverse an apparently foregone conclusion.

Thompson a member of the school's first eighth-grade class and subsequently a Harrison School teacher was incensed at the possibility that her alma mater might be torn down. Already in her 70s she nevertheless galvanized a grassroots campaign to save the building and, says Reynolds, pressed from the outset for creation of a Black cultural center. Hazel Thompson died in 1988.

Now Harrison is a trend setter once more, as the Harrison Heritage and Cultural Center is in the forefront of preserving Black heritage in the Roanoke Valley.

Documenting the achievements and culture of the Black community is a primary focus of the Harrison Center, which is building a collection of objects, photographs, and records so future generations can appreciate those who went before.

Hampton

>University Museum
>Hampton University
>Hampton, Virginia 23668
>(804) 727-5308

On the historic Hampton University campus is one of America's remarkable museums, founded in 1868, the University Museum is among the oldest museums in Virginia. Its collection contains art and artifacts from cultures and nations around the world. With over 6,000 objects and works of art, Hampton University has the largest and strongest collection of its kind in the southeastern United States.

A visit to the University Museum begins with an appreciation of the significant history of a unique educational institution. Hampton was founded in 1868 for the education of newly freed Black Americans. The museum is housed in Academy Building, a National Historic Landmark dedicated in 1881. Like all of the University's older buildings, Hampton Institute students and faculty built this four-story brick and stucco structure.

Best known and most sought after by scholars, researchers, and the public is the African collection. Today it numbers about 2,000 pieces representing 87 ethnic groups, and cultures. Acquired by the University in 1911, the first 400 objects in this collection were gathered between 1890 and 1910 by the missionary- explorer, Dr. William H. Sheppard, who had been a student at Hampton in the 1880's. While the Sheppard Collection is recognized widely as outstanding by any measure, since its 1911 acquisition, numerous gifts from African students, other missionaries, friends and faculty of the University and distinguished private collectors have created a most significant resource representing all culture areas and geographic regions of Africa.

Alexandria

Alexandria Black History
Alexandria Resource Center
Box 178 - City Hall
Alexandria, Virginia 22314
(703) 838-4356

The building that today houses the Alexandria Black History Resource Center was constructed in 1940, as the Black community's first public library. With desegregation in the 1960s the building was converted to use for community service programs.

Due to the efforts of the Parker-Gray School Alumni Association and the Society for the Preservation of Black Heritage, Inc., the building reopened in 1983 as the Alexandria Black History Resource Center. The Parker-Gray Alumni Association, the Society for the Preservation of Black Heritage, and the Friends of Black History, provided staffing for the center. In 1987, City Council placed the operation of the center under the direction of the Office of Historic Alexandria and provided funding for paid staff.

The Black History Resource Center presents lectures, walking tours and other activities relating to the history and accomplishments of blacks in Alexandria. Painting, Photographs, books and other memorabilia document the Black experience in Alexandria and Virginia from 1749 to the present. A permanent exhibition explores the role of Blacks in nineteenth and twentieth-century Alexandria. The center has a special collection on the history and graduates of the Parker-Gray School.

Richmond

Maggie Walker National Historic Site
c/o National Park Service
3215 E. Broad Street
Richmond, VA 23223
(804) 226-1981
Home of black leader banker
Champion of self-help initiatives
Site 110-1/2 East Leigh Street

The Maggie L. Walker National Historic Site in Richmond, Virginia commemorates the life of an unusually gifted woman. Despite being female, Black, and physically handicapped, she achieved success in the world of business and finance. Under her direction and guidance the Independent Order of St. Luke expanded from a fraternal beneficial society to an insurance company, owning a newspaper and a bank (of which she was editor and president respectively), and a department store. The bank, the St. Luke Penny Savings Bank, continues today as Consolidated Bank and Trust, the oldest surviving block-operated bank in the United States. In addition, she was active in civic groups, fostering racial cohesiveness and improved economic and educational opportunities for her people.

The St. Luke Herald newspaper was established in 1901 under Mrs. Walker's editorship to promote closer communication between the order and the public. Two years later the St. Luke Penny Savings Bank was founded. She had earlier stated, Let us put our money together; let us use our money; let us put our money out at usury among ourselves and reap the benefit ourselves". Mrs. Walker served as the bank's first president. The bank survives today as the oldest continually Black-operated bank in the United States.

Maggie (Mitchell) Walker was born in Richmond, Virginia to Elizabeth Draper near the close of the Civil War. Her mother, a former slave, was the cook's helper in the Van Lew Mansion. Later, Elizabeth Draper and her husband William Mitchell moved their family to a small house in a downtown alley between Broad and Marshall, where Maggie and her brother Johnnie were raised.

Maggie Mitchell joined the local independent order of St. Luke. This fraternal insurance society established in 1867. <u>The St. Luke Herald</u> newspaper was established in 1901 under Mrs. Walker's editorship to promote closer communication between the order and the public. Two years later the St. Luke Penny Savings Bank was founded.

CHAPTER 4

Be as proud of your race today as our Fathers were in the Days of yore. We have a beautiful history, and we shall create another in the future that will astonish the world.

Marcus Garvey

HISTORICAL SOCIETIES

Connecticut Afro-American Historical Society, Inc.
444 Orchard Street
New Haven, Connecticut 06511
(203) 776-4907

Afro-American Historical Society of Delaware
512 East Fourth Street
Wilmington, Delaware 19801
(302) 984-1423

Afro-American Genealogical and Historical Society
DuSable Museum
740 East 56th Place
Chicago, Illinois 60637
(312) 947-0600
Toni Costonie

Robbins Historical Society
P.O. Box 1561
Robbins, Illinois 60472

Indiana African-American Historical Genealogical Society
502 Clover Terrace
Bloomington, Indiana 47404-1809
(812) 332-5132

Afro-American Historical Society
P.O. Box 3151
834 Pottawatumie Street
Forth Leavenworth, Kansas 66048
(913) 651-4584

Egyptian Historical Society
New Creation Lutheran Church
2111 West Broadway
Louisville, Kentucky 40211-1001

Afro-American Historical and Cultural Society of Jersey City
1841 Kennedy Boulevard
Jersey City, New Jersey 07305
(201) 547-5262

Afro-American Historical Society of the Niagara Frontier
P.O. Box 1663
Buffalo, New York 14216
(716) 694-5096

Westchester African-American Historical Society
1126 Howard Street
Pee Skill, New York 10566
(914) 737-2606

Afro-American Cultural and Historical Society Museum
1765 Crawford Road
P.O. Box 20039
Cleveland, Ohio 44120
(216) 791-1700

Tarrant County Black Historical and Genealogical Society, Inc.
1020 East Humboldt Street
Forth Worth, Texas 76104
(817) 332-6049

Black Heritage Society of Washington State, Inc.
P.O. Box 22565
Seattle, Washington 98122

Wisconsin Black Historical Society/Museum
P.O. Box 11887
Milwaukee, Wisconsin 53211
(414) 449-3824

GENEALOGICAL SOCIETIES

Arizona Chapter AAHGs
P.O. Box 83434
Phoenix, Arizona 85071-3434

California African American Genealogical Society
2526 - 4th Avenue
Los Angeles, California 90018-1712

Afro-American Historical and Genealogical Society, Inc.
P.O. Box 73086
Washington, D.C. 20056-3086

Central Florida Chapter AAHGs
P.O. Box 5742
Deltona, Florida 32728

Little Egypt Chapter AAHGs
908 Burton Street
Carbondale, Illinois 62901

Patricia Liddell Researchers
Chicago Chapter AAHGs
460 East 41st Street #917
Chicago, Illinois 60653

Central Maryland
Chapter - AAHGs
P.O. Box 2774
Columbia, Maryland 21045

National Capitol Area
Chapter AAHGs
7808 Berry Place
Forestville, Maryland 20747

Baltimore Chapter AAHGs
P.O. Box 66265
Baltimore, Maryland 21239

Fred Hart Williams Genealogical Society
5201 Woodward Avenue
Detroit, Michigan 48202

New Jersey Chapter AAHGs
124 Mount Salem Road
Wantage, New Jersey 07461

Jean Sampson Scott
Greater New York Chapter AAHGs
P.O. Box 022340
Brooklyn, New York 11202

North Carolina AAHGs
P.O. Box 26785
Raleigh, North Carolina 27611-6785

Cleveland Chapter AAHGs
P.O. Box 200382
Cleveland, Ohio 44120-9998

AA Genealogy Group of The AA
Historical and Cultural Museum
7th and Arch Streets
Philadelphia, Pennsylvania 19106

Texas State Chapter AAHGs
P.O. Box 670045
Houston, Texas 77267-0045

HISTORICAL ORGANIZATIONS

Community on Black Pioneers - Alton Museum
121 East Broadway
Alton, Illinois 62002
(618) 462-2763
(618) 462-1943
Grace Monroe, President

Bloomington - Normal Black History Project
Illinois State University
University Museum
Normal, Illinois 61761-6901
(309) 438-8800
(309) 452-1757

Association for the Study of Afro-American Life and History
The Carter G. Woodson Center
1401 4th Street, N.W.
Washington, D.C. 20005
(202) 667-2822

Black Heritage Tours
Bureau of Publicity and Information
532 South Perry Street
Montgomery, Alabama 36130
(205) 832-5510

Association for the Study of Afro-American Life and History
Black Heritage Trail Tour
Georgia Department of Industry and Trade
P.O. Box 1776
Atlanta, Georgia 30301-1776

African-American Museums Association
420 Seventh Street, N.W.
Washington, D.C. 20004
(202) 783-7744

Black Civil War Tribute Committee
2814 Buena Vista Pike
Nashville, Tennessee 37218
(615) 254-0970

Middle Tennessee Conference Afro-American Scholars
Tennessee State University
Nashville, Tennessee
(615) 320-3200
Mailing address: P.O. Box 130
Department of Geography and History
Nashville, Tennessee 37203

Afro-American Heritage Association
P.O. Box 451
Rome, New York 13440
(315) 337-5018

Black Revolutionary War Patriots Foundation
1612 K Street, N.W., Suite 1104
Washington, D.C. 20006
(202) 939-8337
(202) 452-1776

Harriet Tubman Association of Dorchester
P.O. Box 25
Cambridge, Maryland 21613-0025
(301) 228-0788

Black Catholic History Resource Center
Archdiocese of Washington, Office of Black Catholics
5001 Eastern Avenue, Room 248
P.O. Box 29260
Washington, D.C., 20017
(301) 853-3800 - Ext. 294

Black Education and Cultural History, Inc.
132 Glenwood Avenue
Portland, Maine 04103
(207) 772-6098
Gerald E. Talbot

The Associations for the Study of Classical African Civilizations
3624 Country Club Drive
Los Angeles, California 90019
(213) 730-1155

Association of African Historians
700 East Oakwood Boulevard
Chicago, Illinois 60653
(312) 268-7500
Dr. Anderson Thompson, President

The Association for the Study of Ancient African Civilizations
Midwest Region
700 East Oakwood Boulevard
Chicago, Illinois 60653
(312) 268-0863

Community for Afro-American History Observances
P.O. Box 1507
Georgetown, South Carolina 29442
(803) 527-2392

African Heritage Studies Association
C/o Ofuctey Kudjoe
Department of Political Studies
Queens College
65-30 Kissena Boulevard
Flushing, New York 11367
(718) 520-2878 - (718) 520-7416

African Studies Association
C/o Dr. Edna Bay
Credit Union Building
Emory University
Atlanta, Georgia 30322
(404) 329-6410

African Studies Association
255 Kinsey Hall
University of California at Los Angeles
Los Angeles, California 90024
(213) 206-8011

Still Family Historical Committee
137 E. Oak Avenue
Lawnside, New Jersey 08045

Exodusters Awareness Incorporated
638 Carnahan Topeka
Topeka, Kansas 66607

Afro-American in New York Life and History
P.O. Box 1663
Buffalo, New York 14216

Afro-American Historical and Genealogical Society
P.O. Box 73086
Washington, D.C. 20056
(202) 829-1205

The Journal of Negro History
P.O. Box 721
Moorehouse College
Atlanta, Georgia 30314

Journal of Negro History
1401 14th Street, N.W.
Washington, D.C. 20005

Open Hand Publisher
P.O. Box 22048
Seattle, Washington 98122
(206) 323-3868

Africana Studies and Research Center
310 Triphammer Road
Ithaca, New York 14850

Journal of African Civilization
Africana Studies Department
Beck Hall
Rutgers University
New Brunswick, New Jersey 08903

UCLA Center for Afro-American Studies
405 Hillgard Avenue
3111 Campbell Hall
Los Angeles, California 90034

BLACK MEMORABILIA

Lewis & Blalock Collection
P.O. Box 28561
Washington, D.C. 20005
(202) 332-3082
Contact: Steve Lewis

Mrs. Ola Mae Johnson's Black Historical/Memorabilia Society
P.O. Box 2250
Gardena, California 90247
(213) 757-4521 (213) 779-4344
Contact: Mrs. Ola Mae Johnson

National Black Memorabilia
Collector's Association
P.O. Box 4556
Upper Marlboro, Maryland 20775
(301) 649-7610
Contact: Maureen Brown

BMCA (Black Memorabilia Collectors' Association
2482 Devoe Ter.
Bronx, N.Y. 10468
(212) 946-1281

UNICA (Universal Intelligence Cosmic Awareness
Malinda Saunders
5406 Ninth St. N. W.
Washington, D. C. 20011
(202) 726-8931

BLACK MILITARY HISTORY

Black Military History Society
1793 Geary Boulevard
San Francisco, California 94115

Black Military History Institute of America, Inc.
C/o Col. William A. DeShields
404 Golf Course Court
Arnold, Maryland 21012
(312) 757-4250
Mailing address:
P.O. Box 1134
Fort Meade, Maryland 20755-0993

ASSOCIATIONS

Frederick Douglass Memorial and Historical Association
14th and W Street, S.W.
Washington, D.C. 20020

Carter G. Woodson Foundation
P.O. Box 1025
Newark, New Jersey 07101
(201) 371-8071
Director: Philip Thomas

NAACP Historical & Cultural Project
441 Bergen Avenue
Jersey City, New Jersey 07304

Afro-American Cultural Foundation
P.O. Box 587
White Plains, New York 10602

Afro-Americans Cultural Center, Inc.
2191 Adam Clayton Powell, Jr., Boulevard
New York, New York 10027
(212) 996-3333 Director: Simon Bly, Jr.

Black History Exhibit Center
106 North Main Street
Hempstead, New York 11550

AFRICAN-AMERICAN LIBRARIES

Birmingham Public and Jefferson County Free Library
Linn-Henley Library for Southern Historical Research
Department of Archives and Manuscripts
2100 Park Place
Birmingham, Alabama 35203
(205) 226-3645

Mobile Public Library
Davis Avenue Branch
564 Davis Avenue
Mobile, Alabama 36603-5916

Prichard Memorial Library
4559 Old Cironelle Highway
Prichard, Alabama 36613
(205) 457-5242

Los Angeles County Public Library
Black Resource Center
150 East El Segundo Boulevard
Los Angeles, California 90061
(213) 538-3350

Los Angeles Public Library
Social Science and Technology Department
630 West Fifth Street
Los Angeles, California 90071
(213) 626-7461

Oakland Public Library
History/Literature Division
125 - 14th Street
Oakland, California 94612   (510) 238-4980

Blair-Caldwell African American Research Library
2401 Welton St.
Denver, Colorado 80205
(720) 865-2401

District of Columbia Public Library
Black Studies Division
Martin Luther King Memorial Library
901 G Street, N.W.
Washington, D.C. 20001
(202) 727-1111 or 727-1211 (202) 727-0321 (Tape)

Joseph E. Lee
Memorial Library-Museum
1424 East 17th Street
Jacksonville, Florida 32206-3343
(904) 358-2096

Atlanta-Fulton Public Library
Special Collections Department
1 Margaret Mitchell Square
Atlanta, Georgia 30303
(404) 730-1700

Johnson Publishing Company
820 South Michigan Ave.
Chicago, Illinois 60605
(312) 322-9200

Carter G. Woodson Regional Library
Chicago Public Library
9525 South Halsted Street
Chicago, Illinois 60628
(312) 747-6900
(312) 745-2080

Enoch Pratt Free Library
Afro-American Collection of Reference Books
The Maryland Room
400 Cathedral Street
Baltimore, Maryland 21201-4484
(301) 396-5468

Prince George's County Memorial Library System
Sojourner Truth Room
6200 Oxon Hill Road
Oxon Hill, Maryland 20745
(301) 839-2400

Detroit Public Library
The Azalia Hackley Memorial Collection
5201 Woodward Avenue
Detroit, Michigan 48202-4007
(313) 833-1480

Minneapolis Public Library and Information Center
Huttner Abolition and Anti-Slavery Collection
300 Mcollet Mall
Minneapolis, Minnesota 55401
(612) 372-6522

Kansas City Public Library
311 East 12th Street
Kansas City, Missouri 64104

St. Louis Public Library
Julia Davis Collection
4415 Natural Bridge Avenue
St. Louis, Missouri 63115

Newark Public Library
Humanities Division
5 Washington Street
Box 630
Newark, New Jersey 07101-0630
(201) 733-7820

Countee Cullen Branch
New York Public Library
104 West 136th Street
New York, New York 10030-2601

Named for the famous Harlem poet, this branch has an auditorium art gallery, and the James Weldon-Johnson Collection of Children's Books. It is on the site of the home of Madame C.J. Walker, one of New York's first black millionaires.

Cleveland Public Library
Martin Luther King, Jr. Branch
1962 Stokes Boulevard
Cleveland, Ohio 4416
(216) 623-7018

Kent Public Library
Art Tatum Cultural Center
3101 Collingwood Blvd.
Toledo, Ohio 43610
(419) 259-5340 Fax (419) 243-6536

Free Library of Philadelphia/ Logan Square Branch
Social Studies and History Department
1333 Wagner Ave.
Philadelphia, Pennsylvania 19141-2916

Fort Worth Public Library
Southeast Branch
4300 East Berry
Fort Worth, Texas 76105

Houston Public Library
Specials Collections Department
500 McKinney Avenue
Houston, Texas 77002
(713) 236-1313

Seattle Public Library
Douglass-Truth Library
23rd Avenue and East Yerler Way
Seattle, Washington 98122
(206) 684-4704

Martin Luther King, Jr. Library
310 West Locust Street
Milwaukee, Wisconsin 33212-2345
(414) 278-3098

LIVING HISTORY PERFORMING GROUPS

"Freetown Village"
617 Indiana Street P.O. Box 1041
Indianapolis, Indiana 46206 -1041
(317) 631-1870

Queens Historical Society
Q.H.S. P.O. Box 7204
Atlanta, Georgia 30309
(404) 763-3374
(213) 971-8182

Queens Historical Society (Q.H.S.) dedicated to the preservation of African royal history and culture was founded by Ingrid Thomas an accomplished fashion historian and designer.

Forty Acres and A Mule, Inc.
8629 Colfax
Detroit, Michigan 48204
899-3110
Rev. Major C. Brown, Sr., President

40 Acres and a Mule, the sage of Black America, a historical account of a Black slave's family struggle for freedom during the Post-Civil war period A promise of 40 acres and a mule, prompted blacks to fight with the Union Army. It was an empty promise. 40 acres and a mule are their tragic story and our continuing struggle. This production 40 acres and a mule asks, "Where's the Beef? - 40 Acres and a Mule!"

Buffalo Soldiers, Inc.
5256 B Larchwood Avenue
Philadelphia, Pennsylvania 19143-1523
(215) 748-5530

Seabrook Village Foundation inc.
Trade Hill Road
RFD 1 Box 225
Midway, Georgia 31320
 (912) 884 – 7008   Fax (912) 884 – 7005

AFRICAN-AMERICAN FILM ORGANIZATIONS

Black Film Center/Archive
Department of Afro-American Studies
Memorial Hall East
Indiana University
Bloomington, Indiana 47405
(812) 335-3874
(812) 335-2684
Director: Pavlus R. Klotman
Assistant Director Gloria J. Gibson - Hudson

The Black Film Center/Archive

The Black Film Center/Archive (BFC/A) is a repository of Black Films and related materials. Black Films include those, which have substantial participation by Afro-Americans as writers, actors, producers, directors, musicians and consultants, as well as those, which depict some aspect of Black experience.

The Black Film Center/Archive preserves Black Films in a safe, temperature controlled environment to prevent loss and deterioration. All films given to the Center/Archive will be catalogued and made available for screening and study.

A precious part of America's cultural heritage, films by and about Blacks, has been rapidly disappearing due to technical indifference to preservation, the lack of established outlets for these films, and inadequate teaching and study resources. Most Americans therefore remain unaware of the social and historic importance of Black Film.

Afro-Americans wrote, directed, produced and starred in films as early as 1916. During the 1920s, 30s, and 40s, independent Black and White filmmakers produced hundreds of films especially for segregated movie houses across the nation. Black filmmakers, like the Johnson brothers and Oscar Micheaux, attempted to create new Black images to counteract the old stereotypes rampant in Hollywood films. These films, and all others with a substantial Black presence, represented a remarkable contribution to American culture.

Objectives
- To expand the film collection of historic and current films by and about Blacks,
- To undertake and to encourage new research in the history, meaning and aesthetics of Black films,
- To train graduate students and research assistants in Black film studios, as well as public school teachers and community leaders,
- To implement an outreach program to provide screening discussions for community organizations, high schools, and other universities and colleges,
- To encourage the continuation of creative film activity by independent Black filmmakers through an annual film festival and workshop.

Current Holdings

Norma Motion Picture Collection
MGM/UA
Paramount Pictures
Warner Brothers

Black American Cinema Society
C/o WSBRC
3617 Montclair Street
Los Angeles, California 90018
(213) 737-3292

Black Film Institute
University of the District of Columbia
Carnegie Building
8th Street and Mt. Vernon Place, N.W.
Washington, D.C. 20001
(202) 727-2396

Black Film Makers Foundation
80 - 8th Avenue, Suite 1704
New York, New York 10011
(212) 927-7771
(212) 924-1198

Traveling Museums

African American Museum
Stephanie Hordge
5809 Winston Dr.
Indianapolis, Indiana 46226   (317) 545-6165

The Black Inventions Museum
P.O. Box 76122
Los Angles, California 90076   (310) 859 – 4602 Founder & Curator – Lady Sala S.Shabazz

Museum of Black Inventors
7 South Newstead Ave.
St. Louis Missouri 63108   (314) 533-1333   Fax (314) 519-0794

CHAPTER 5

*Before Africa can unite
Africa must unite*

"It took an educational effort that was systematic, intensive, and unparalleled in the History of the World to erase these memories, to cloud vision, to impair hearing, and to impede the operation of the critical capacities among African American. Once reference points were lost, African Americans as a people became like a computer without a program, a spacecraft without a homing device, a dependent without a benefactor."

- Asa G. Hilliard III

AFRICAN-AMERICAN SUBJECT RELATED MUSEUMS

Uncle Remus Museum
360 Oak Street Hwy 4415
Eatonton, Georgia 31024
P.O. Box 184
(404) 485-6856
Founded, 1963

Eatonton also has a famous creature, Br'er Rabbit. Writer Joel Chandler Harris was born and developed his famous Uncle Remus stories here. The Uncle Remus Museum replicates the slave cabin where Br'er Rabbit came to life and exhibits "de critters" of Uncle Remus, as well as first editions of many of Harris' works.

As a boy, Harris was associated with old slaves whose gift for storytelling he was later able to duplicate in unforgettable tales of his own.

Harriet Beecher Stowe House & Museum
2950 Gilbert Avenue
Cincinnati, Ohio 45206
(513) 221-0004

While she drew upon her remarkable memory of childhood incidents and people for her early writings, Harriet recharged her mind with observations of her new surroundings. Cincinnati was one of the starting points of the Underground Railroad. Reverend John Rankin has been helping fugitive slaves escape. It was his account of a Negro named Eliza, who braved the thawing ice of the Ohio River in her escape that provided Harriet with Eliza of Uncle Tom's Cabin. Hearing Reverend Josiah Henson, an ex-slave speak in 1851, at Brunswick, Maine, motivated her to write her famous novel; it was he who provided the character, Uncle Tom. Her masterful use of Negro dialect, the childhood tales of her Aunt Esther, once married to a slave owner in Jamaica and letters from her brother Charles, about cruel plantation owners he met while traveling on the Mississippi, all contributed to her book. The novel eclipsed the efforts of the abolitionists.

Fort Concho
213 East Avenue O
San Angelo, Texas 76903
(915) 657-4441
(915) 655-9121 Ext. 441

This museum features Buffalo Soldiers and sponsors a Buffalo Soldier reenactment unit. The Fort Concho Buffalo Soldiers unit re-creates the lives of Black cavalrymen on the Texas frontier. The unit can be seen at Fort Concho during Christmas at Old Fort Concho Buffalo Soldiers unit takes part in the living history.

Simpson's Collection at Wadsworth Atheneum
The Amistad Foundation
600 Main Street
Hartford, Connecticut 06103
(203) 278-2760

The Simpson is one of the world's outstanding records of the Black experience in America. It consists of more than 6,000 objects and is housed in the Wadsworth Atheneum, America's oldest public art museum in Hartford, Connecticut. The collection is under the management of The Amistad Foundation, which was formed by the Atheneum as a unique approach to maximize the accessibility to this historic treasure and to utilize this important national cultural asset.

What is the Simpson Collection?

The Simpson Collection is unparallel as it documents over three centuries of the Black experience in America. As a cultural asset, The Simpson Collection is exceptional in many ways. From the slave chains of the Middle Passage to the extraordinary contributions made by Black Americans to art, science, social science, politics, literature and history, it is a powerful testimony and a rich resource in the study of Black American history and America's institutions.

The Collection is intentionally and predominately graphic. Paintings, sculpture, prints, various kinds of popular art and photographs present starting images of Black American life. These are intensely evocative of not only the experience of Black Americans, but also of their many contributions to American culture.

The library enhances the visual impact. It is unique in that the art collection is augmented by historical documents such as letters, slave contracts, autograph manuscripts, broadsides, and more than 350 books. It thus sets forth an important aspect of the American heritage with unusual thoroughness. The collection is a powerful testimony and a rich resource for the study of Black American history.

The strength of the collection lies in its more than 2200 photographs. They range from vivid images of slave life in the early 1840s to some of the most memorable news photos from our own time.

All of the photographic media of the 19th and 20th centuries are included, providing a history of photography itself - daguerreotypes, ambrotypes, cartes de Vista, tintypes, cabinets and stereopticon views. Some are the work of prominent photographers such as Matthew Brady and others are by notable Black photographers such as Augustus Washington and Thomas Ball. Altogether they are an incomparable record extending from prominent personalities to images of industry, education and the everyday life of ordinary, dignified Black Americans.

There are many great varieties, including an autographed photograph of Booker T. Washington in the year he became the first principal of Tuskegee Institute.

Another significant aspect of the Simpson collection is the number of objects actually owned by slaves or used in the slave trade.

The Black experience is revealed across every artistic medium from fold art to advertising. Unusual depictions of Blacks in cartoons, postcards, humorous pamphlets, and sheet music of minstrel songs offer vivid testimony of racial attitudes and valuable insight into American race relations.

Balch Institute for Ethnic Studies
18 South Seventh Street
Philadelphia, Pennsylvania 19106
(215) 925-8090

Holdings for the Balch Institute

**General
Manuscript Collections**

American Friends Service Committee. Case files, ca. 1933-1952, concerning the plight of refugees from Eastern Europe.	(R) 175 cartons
Magdalen Society, Philadelphia. Records, 1826-1921	6 rolls
Methodist Church Conferences. Records, 1800-1960	27 rolls
New York City. Police Department. Records, 1863, 1865-1866, of the twelfth precinct.	2 volumes
Philadelphia Fellowship Commission. Papers, 1945-1967. Unprocessed. (R)	1 carton
Rev. Eugene Runtagh. Papers, 1910-1937, concerning St. Mary's Greek Catholic Church, Nesquehoning, Pa., and St. Martin Archangel Church, Dunmore, Pa., of which he was pastor.	1 folder
Steamship Passenger Lists, 1899-1900, primarily of Dutch and German immigrants.	2 folders
Works Progress Administration. Ethnic Survey of Pennsylvania, 1938-1941	8 rolls

**Afro-American
Manuscript Collections**

American Colonization Society. Records, 1792-1964	323 rolls
Paul Dunbar. Papers, 1873-1942	9 rolls
Albert E. Dutrieuille. Papers, ca. 1914-1974, of a Philadelphia caterer and restaurant owner. Unprocessed. (R)	2 boxes

Maryland Colonization Society.

Records, 1827-1902   31 rolls

William Moore. Papers, 1871-ca. 1952, of a
Philadelphia-born tennis player and teacher.
Unprocessed.   1 box

Negro Public Library, Tyler, Texas.
Records, 1920-1960   1 box

Henry C. Patterson. Papers, 1929-1972, of
a civil rights advocate and the first Philadelphia
director of the United Negro College Fund.   1 box

St. Peter Claver Church, Philadelphia.
Records, 1877-1954   1 folder - 3 rolls

James S. Stemons. Papers, 1894-1922, of a
proponent of Afro-American rights, lecturer,
and editor of two Philadelphia newspapers.   3 boxes

Bascom Warley and Sons, Upholsterers, Philadelphia.
Records, 1903-1910   1 volume

Works Progress Administration. Slave Narrative
Collection, 1936-1938   11 rolls

Colonial Williamsburg's Historic Area
Carter's Grove Plantation
(Slave Quarter)
Williamsburg, Virginia

    The opening of the slave quarter marks the first time a major museum has interpreted the challenging issue of slave life in the colonial Chesapeake on any original site. the reconstruction of the quarter, including three slave houses, a corncrib, and a tobacco barn, provides new interpretive opportunities for colonial Williamsburg.
    This project also fulfills Colonial Williamsburg's objective to take a pro-active approach to the teaching of colonial Black history.

Levi Coffin State Historic Site
P.O. Box 77
U.S. Route 27
Fountain City, Indiana 47341
(317) 847-2432

Life for a runaway slave was full of hazards. Without maps, the North Star served as the only direction of freedom. Traveling only a few miles each night, slaves had to beware of search parties, empowered by the passage of the Fugitive Slave Law in 1850.

To the thousands of Blacks fleeing slavery, an eight-room Federal type brick home in Newport (Fountain City), Indiana became a safe haven on their journey. This was the home of Lewis and Catherine Coffin, North Carolina Quakers, who opposed slavery. During the 20 years they lived in Newport, the Coffins help 2,000 escaped slaves reach safety.

It was not just the Coffins who helped., the entire town of 30 families contributed to the cause. Neighbor women often made clothes for the slaves, as well as cooked. Once in the house, the slaves were concealed for up to several weeks, until they regained enough strength to continue their journey.

In their flight, slaves used three main routes to cross into freedom. Cincinnati, Madison and Jeffersonville. From these points, the fugitives were taken by boat or trail to Newport. After their stay at the Coffin house, they went on, sometimes as far as Canada. So successful was the Coffin sanctuary that while they operated in Newport, not a single slave given assistance, failed to reach freedom. One of the many slaves, who were given sanctuary by the Coffins, was "Eliza," whose story is told in Uncle Tom's Cabin.

Delta Blues Museum
114 Delta Avenue
P.O. Box 280
Clarksdale, Mississippi 38614
(601) 624-4461

The blues heritage is alive and well in its birthplace; Clarksdale, Mississippi. America's unique form of music, the blues, began in the Mississippi Delta. Clarksdale and Coahoma County were home to famed blues-men W.C. Handy, Charlie Patton, Robert Johnson, Son House, Muddy Waters, Howlin' Wolf, John Lee Hooker and many others whose music continues to entertain and inspire millions of people around the world.

The blues also importantly influenced jazz, country, rock and roll and popular music. The museum attempts to increase understanding and appreciation of the blues and the blues' intricate relationship with these and other forms of music and American culture.

The 1979, the Carnegie Public Library Board of Trustees established the Blue Museum as a division of its organization for the purpose of collecting preserving and making accessible to the public information comprising the historic and significance of the blues.

Kentucky Derby Museum
At Churchill Downs
704 Central Avenue
P.O. Box 3513
Louisville, Kentucky 40201
(502) 637-1111

Black jockeys played a vital role in shaping early American turf history and the Kentucky Derby is no exception. Fourteen of the 15 riders in the first derby were Black while Black reins men won 15 of the derby's first 28 runnings.

On June 25, 1980, the NAACP and the Lincoln Foundation honored the 11 Black jockeys who rode a total of 15 derby winners between 1875 and 1902. A plaque commemorating the occasion is now on display in the Kentucky Derby Museum.

Black Jockey Winners

Oliver Lewis	James Winkfield	Babe Hurd
William Walker	James "Soup" Perkins	Issac Murphy
Erskin Henderson	Alonzo Clayton	
George Lewis	Issac Lewis	

Thompson-Hickman Library
Highway 287
Virginia City, Montana 59755
(406) 843-5346

Permanent collection includes materials on Black cowboys and miners active during the heyday of Virginia City. A prominent Black figure covered is Stephen Bickford, who established on the City's early waterworks.

Old Slave House (Crenshaw House)
Route 1 and 13 - Gallatin County
Equality, Illinois 62954
(618) 276-4410

The mansion stands on its hilltop, nine miles west of Old Shawneetown, overlooking the Saline River Valley. The house itself is not important, but what happened inside the house is connected to Illinois Black history and legendary slave traffic.

John Hart Crenshaw, a wealthy white man, owned the house and the salt mines. He had slaves work in the salt mines.

John Crenshaw has other business interests. He has experience in dealing with slaves through legal channels and illegal channels. Blacks who came to Illinois with certified papers that showed they were freemen, found themselves at Hickory Hill. That was the name John Crenshaw called the house. Others called it the Old Slave House. It was common practice to make raids on these freemen and hold them to sell across the river into slavery.

They wanted to keep the captives hidden until their searchers gave up looking form them, then they would ship them across into slavery territory. There are many tales of what happened on the third floor of Hickory Hill-Old Slave House.

We do know that John Crenshaw leased slaves from Kentucky and Missouri owners and that he apprenticed or bound others. He was also charged with kidnapping free Negroes and selling them into slavery. The case was tried at the spring term of court in 1842. Mr. Crenshaw was acquitted, which might have been due to his innocence or to his financial and political eminence.

One of the most frequently told stories deals with Crenshaw's attempt to breed slaves and sell the young babies as soon as they could be weaned from their mother's breasts. For this purpose, it is said; he imported a male or buck Negro from the south by the name of Bob, whose record in begetting strong and health offspring was remarkable. In the slave quarters was his special room into which captive female slaves were forced. Whatever the truth of these stories, there exists today the darkout and referred to as "The Breeding Room" or "Uncle Bob's Room."

The Stagville Center
P.O. Box 71217
Oxford Highway
Durham, North Carolina 27722-1217
(919) 620-0120

Stagville today is a 71-acre historic property owned by the State of North Carolina and located in the northern section of Durham County.

Stagville Center operates under the authority of the Division of Archives and History of the North Carolina Department of Cultural Resources. The non-profit Stagville Center Corporation provides further support. Together with the Stagville Center Corporation, the friends of Stagville and the Stagville Associates provide special funding and handsome help with Stagville programming.

The North Carolina plantation holdings of the Bennehan-Cameron family were among the largest of the pre-civil war south. Approximately 900 slaves worked that land, which totaled almost 30,000 acres by 1860. Stagville, a plantation of several thousand acres, lay at the center of this enormous estate.

Where did the slaves come from?

The slaves who were brought to America, and whose descendants labored at Stagville, were generally of West African origin. Although united by certain common beliefs, enslaved Africans came from many different cultures, which stretched across a wide geographical area. Africans became united by color only after they were captives and transported to America.

Slaves general came from agrarian societies including the Ibo, Eve, Biafada, Bokongo, Wolog, Bambara and Werer people, societies that were predominately family based socially, politically and economically. Slave raiders did, not usually invade the large African cities and states with standing armies.

The eighteenth center was the most crucial time for slaves because their increasing numbers enabled them to form communities and combine various cultural remnants from Africa into a new, viable African-American culture. Stagville plantation reflects some of this African culture in America.

Rankin House
P.O. Box 176
219 North Second Street
Ripley, Ohio 45167
(513) 392-1627
(513(392-4377

The epitaph on the granite monument reads simply "freedom's heroes." They were freedom's heroes, John and Jean Rankin, but the tyranny against which they fought to save the United States was a tyranny from within. They had thrown down the gauntlet at the doorstep of their home, overlooking the Ohio River at Ripley, and dared anyone to stop them. During the 40-year period, 1825 to 1865, they and their Brown County neighbors sheltered more than 2,000 slaves escaping to freedom. The stories of fear and daring recanted before the hearth of the Rankin home, inspired some to join in the struggle, and others most notably Lyman Beecher's daughter, Harriet Beecher Stowe - to dramatize the battle and focus the attention of the world on the problem of slavery.

John Rankin, Presbyterian minister and educator, had begun his battle against slavery years before the building of his Liberty Hill home, near Ripley. He has preached the abolitionist view as early as 1815. His series of 13 letters denouncing the peculiar institution were published in book form as Letters on American Slavery, in 1826.

The letters helped to build sentiment against slavery and aided Rankin in organizing anti-slavery groups on a local and state level. Rankin believes it to be the responsibility of the Federal Government to purchase slaves from their masters and set them free.

It was unavoidable that the Rankin house would sooner or later become a stopping point on the Underground Railroad. Slaves had been escaping to freedom in the North since before the Revolution. The Ordinance of 1787, prohibiting slavery in the Northwest Territory, made this a particularly desirable haven.

Rankin, his wife and fellow sympathizers became conductors on the Underground Railroad in the 1820's. As the trickle of escaped slaves swelled to a floodtide, others joined in the complex underground organization. Ministers, teamsters, blacksmiths, clerks, farmers and steamboat men all became part of the struggle.

The task became more difficult with the passage of the Fugitive Slave Act of 1850, under which slaves could be captured in free territory and returned to their masters if ownership could be established. Anyone having a runaway was subject to a heavy fine. Since each slave frequently represented a substantial cash value, many owners were relentless in their pursuit. Informers and Bounty hunters found a livelihood in the often-sizable rewards offered by Southern owners for return of their "property."

Many ruses were devised to outwit the slave hunter. Secret hiding places were built in houses, barns and stores; an intricate system of alternate routes were established; disguises were used; pursuers were led on many fruitless chases by decoys, false information was confided to eager and unsuspecting owners.

In the meantime, the slaves were hidden, bedded, clothed and sent north to freedom in Canada. The Rankin home at one time had as many as 12 escapees. The family was proud of never having lost a "passenger."

Casey Jones Railroad Museum State Park
10901 Vaughan Rd. #1
Vaughan, Mississippi 39179
(601) 673 – 9864

Less than fifty miles north of Jackson Mississippi is the site of the beginning of a legend. Near Vaughan, Mississippi is the location of the wreck of the Cannonball pulled by Engine No. 382, with the white engineer Johnathan Luther Casey Jones at the throttle. Trying to make up time in the run from Memphis to Canton, Mississippi. Jones has just run through a stop signal when a freight train came into view crossing the tracks in front of the "Cannonball." The Cannonball rammed into four cars of the freight train. Jones was killed in the crash.

The tale of the ill – fated "Cannonball" would have ended on that April night in 1900 if not for a friend of Jones and the popularity of Vanderville. Wallace Saunders, an African – American engine wiper in Water Valley and a friend of Jones, was deeply moved by the engineer's death and composed "The Ballad of Casey Jones" as a tribute to his friend.

Casey Jones admired and respected the men responsible for the upkeep of the locomotives, and he and Saunders has been friends for several years. Saunders had a talent for making up ballads about people and events; he composed the first version of "The Ballad of Casey Jones." He sang this song along with others in his repertoire, on the streets of Canton for anyone who would listen. One of these who listened was William Leighton, an Illinois Central engineer whose two brothers performed vauderville as the Leighton Brothers. Fictional verses were added to the song and it becomes a popular hit. Thanks to a black man by the name of Wallace Saunders.

Savannah History Museum
303 Martin Luther King Jr. Blvd.
Savannah, Georgia 31401-4217

This exhibit highlights the history of African – American soldiers from the Revolutionary War to after World War II. Also highlighted are the first South Carolina Volunteer Infantry and the 178,895 African – American men who fought during the Civil War.

Slavehaven/Underground Railroad
P.O. Box 27146
Memphis, Tennessee. 38167

Also known as the Burkle Estate, Slavehaven was a way station on the Underground Railroad. Today, the more –than – 100-year old house is a museum in Memphis. With nineteenth-century furnishing, Slavehaven is filled with artifacts, memorabilia and historical documents that reflect the harsh realities of slavery. A walk through the seven – room house reveals trap doors and a cellar where slaves hid while awaiting the signal that it was safe to take the journey up North. Guided tours are available for individuals, schools and groups.

CHAPTER 6

*"Though we eat with separate mouths
We feed one belly."*

African……..Proverb

MAJOR CITIES WITHOUT AFRICAN-AMERICAN MUSEUMS

Phoenix, Arizona
San Jose, California
New Haven, Connecticut
Jacksonville, Florida
Honolulu, Hawaii
Gary, Indiana
Wichita, Kansas
Minneapolis, Minnesota
Albuquerque, New Mexico

Raleigh, North Carolina
Winston/Salem, North Carolina
Akron, Ohio
Toledo, Ohio
Youngstown, Ohio
Tulsa, Oklahoma
Portland, Oregon
Pittsburgh, Pennsylvania

SECONDARY CITIES THAT NEED AFRICAN-AMERICAN MUSEUMS

Hobson City, Alabama
Anchorage, Alaska
Fairbanks, Alaska
Juneau, Alaska
Tucson, Arizona
Compton, California
Inglewood, California
Sacramento, California
Dover, Delaware
Columbus, Georgia
Robbins, Illinois
Rockford, Illinois
Rock Island / Moline, Illinois
Springfield, Illinois
Fort Wayne, Indiana
South Bend, Indiana
Vincennes, Indiana
Cedar Rapids, Iowa
Des Moines, Iowa
Topeka, Kansas
Covington, Kentucky

Frankfort, Kentucky
Paducah, Kentucky
Alcorn, Mississippi
Meridian, Mississippi
Mound Bayou, Mississippi
Jefferson City, Missouri
Reno, Nevada
Fayetteville, North Carolina
Columbus, Ohio
East Cleveland, Ohio
Lincoln Heights, Ohio
Boley, Oklahoma
Langston, Oklahoma
Harrisburg, Pennsylvania
York, Pennsylvania
Texarkana, Texas
Petersburg, Virginia
Spokane, Washington
Charleston, West Virginia
Huntington, West Virginia
Racine, Wisconsin

Africa Fact Sheet

- **Nile River** - Longest river in the world
- **Africa** - Second largest continent
- **First** men in the world were born in Africa
- **Sahara Desert** - largest desert in the world
- **Developed** the world's first calendar
- **Built** the first step pyramid
- The oldest tools on record found in **Tanzania**
- **First** physician found in Africa
- **Hippocrates,** Father of modern medicine
- **Ethiopia**, one of the world's oldest nations
- **Colored** - no land, no country
- **Negro**, the Portuguese word meaning black, is the term generally used in the United States to refer to
- **Black People,** - of African origin, but no tie to land (a name without a country).
- **Afro-American** - 1980's term used to identify Americans of African origin, but defines half a person. Correct term: African-American.
- **African** - Black pigmentation, tight curled hair and broad oval noses.

Carter G. Woodson, Historian
Father of African-American History
(1875-1950)

     One of the leading writers on African-American History, Carter Godwin Woodson, was born on December 19, 1875 in New Canton, Virginia. Carter Woodson's parents, Anne Eliza (Riddle) Woodson and James Henry Woodson, were former slaves, who could neither read or write.
     Carter's father made sure his son was serious about his studies. He taught him that when you learn to accept insult to your people, you have lost your soul. Be polite, but insist always on recognition as a human being.
     Carter G. Woodson's interest started when he met a coal miner by the name of Oliver Jones. Oliver could not read the current newspapers and books he had on the Negro, but he paid Carter to read to him. He also gave him food.
     Carter also became friends with some of Jones' co-workers. They discussed the trials and battles of Black people's freedom. This again started Carter's interest in the heritage of Black people.
     In 1895 at 20, Woodson left the mines and enrolled at Douglas High School. Two years later, he was graduating with honors. Carter continued his studies at Berea College in Kentucky and again after two years, returned to Douglas High as its principal. In 1907, he received his Bachelor of Arts degree and in 1908, a Masters of Arts degree from the University of Chicago. In 1912, he earned the degree of Doctor of Philosophy at Howard University.
     During all these years, Carter Woodson was reading and doing research on the Negroes in America and Africa. He was convinced that if a race had no recorded story, its achievements would be forgotten and in time, claimed by other groups. He found that many of the achievements of Negroes were overlooked, ignored, and even suppressed by writers of history textbooks and by the teachers who used them. Woodson's one ambition was that Negro youth should grow up with a firm knowledge of the contributions of the Negro to American history.

"Race prejudice," said Dr. Woodson, "grows naturally from the idea that the Negro race is inferior."

The first book Carter Woodson wrote was *The Education of the Negro Prior to 1861*. Woodson was already recognized as one of the leaders among Black intellectuals. His first papers were never published. Though ridiculed for his aims, Dr. Woodson persisted, and bit by bit, he gathered and sorted information. His monumental recording of the lost and ignored history of the American Negro became the basis for a number of books on the subject.

In 1915, Dr. Woodson organized the Association for the Study of Negro Life and History. Woodson wanted to counteract the influence of the movie, Birth of a Nation, a picture then showing in the theaters. It degraded the Black man and glorified the Ku Klux Klan.

Woodson wanted to reach more children and young people. To do this, he inaugurated an annual celebration, Negro History Week, to be held in February. Negro History Week covers the birth dates of both Abraham Lincoln and Frederick Douglass.

Woodson died April 3, 1950 quietly and unexpectedly during the night, alone in his apartment, above his office at 74 years of age. His funeral was held at Shiloh Baptist Church and he was buried in Lincoln Memorial Cemetery, Suitland, Maryland. Shortly thereafter, a high school in Washington, D.C. was named after him. This scholar, historian, and humanitarian will live longest through his books and his pioneer researches into the history of his race.

Carter G. Woodson Works

- 1915 The Education of the Negro Prior to 1861
- 1918 A Century of Negro Migration
- 1921 The History of the Negro Church
- 1922 The Negro in Our History
- 1924 Free Negro Owners of Slaves in the United States in 1830
- 1925 Free Negro Heads of Families in the United States in 1830
- 1926 The Mind of the Negro as Reflected in Letters Written During the Crisis 1800-1860
- 1928 African Myths together with proverbs: A supplementary reader composed of folk tales from various parts of Africa
- 1929 The Negro as a Businessman
- 1930 The Negro Wage Earner
- 1930 The Rural Negro
- 1933 The Mis-Education of the Negro
- 1934 The Negro Professional Man and the Community
- 1935 The Story of the Negro Retold
- 1936 The African Background Outlined
- 1939 African Heroes and Heroines

Pledge to the Red, Black and Green

This flag is mine,
Here's to this of mine,
The red, black and green,
Hopes in its future bright,
African has been,
Here's to the red of it,
Great nations shall know of it
In time to come.

Red blood shall flow of it,
Great flag of mine.
Here's to the black of it,
Four hundred million back of it,
Whose destiny depends on it,
The red, black and green of it,
Oh flag of mine.

Here's to the green of it,
Young men shall dream of
Maidens shall sing of it,
Waving so high
Here's to the whole of it,
Colors brought and sole of it,
Pleased is my soul with it,
Regardless of what of it,
Thank God for giving,
Great flag of mine.

Lift Every Voice and Sing
Negro National Anthem

Lift every voice and sing, 'till earth and heaven ring
Ring with the harmonies of liberty;
Let our rejoicing rise, high as the listening skies
Let it resound loud as the rolling sea.

Sing a song full of the faith that the dark past has taught us,
Sing a song full of the hope that the present has brought us.

Facing the rising sun, of a new day begun
Let us march on, 'till victory is won!

Stony the road we trod, bitter the chast'ning rod
Felt in the days when hope had died,
Yet with a steady beat, have not our weary feet,
Come to the place for which our fathers sighed?

We have come over a way that tears have been watered,
We have come treading our path through the blood of the slaughtered.

Out from the gloomy past, 'til now we stand at last
Where the white gleam, of our bright star is cast.

God of our weary years, God of our silent tears,
Though who has brought us far on the way
Thou who has by Thy might, lead us into the light,
Keep us forever in the path, we pray.

Lest our feet stray from the places our God, where we met Thee,
Lest our hearts, drunk with the wine of the world, forget Thee.
Shadowed beneath Thy hand, may we forever stand
True to our God, true to our native land.

By James Weldon Johnson

Museum - Books

Establishment of an African-American Heritage. Memorial Museum: Hearing held before the subcommittee on Libraries and Memorials of the committee on House Administration, September 21, 1989, Washington. Washington: U.S., G.P.O., 1990.

The African-American Museum Association. Blacks in the Museum profession. Categorized by areas of expertise. Reference work, 60 p.p. African-American Museum Association 420 7th Street, N.W., Washington, D.C. 20004 (202) 782-7744.

Black American's Information Directory 1990-1991.
Darren L. Smith, Gale Research, Inc., Detroit.

Index to Afro-American Reference Resources compiled by Rosemary M. Stevenson, Greenwood Press 1988.

Afro-American Art Organizations, Art Museums and Art Galleries, in The Complete Annotated Resource Guide to Black American Art. 1978 p.p. 216-239.

The Black Resource Guide, 1984 p.176. "Cultured and Historical Organizations or Museums in The Complete Annotated Resource Guide to Black American Art. 1978. p.p. 241-249.

In Their Footsteps: The American Visions Guide to African – American Heritage Sites by Henry Chase and Henry Holt.

Guide to Black Washington By Sandra Fitzpatrick and Maria Goodwin published Hippocrene.

Black America by Marcella Thum publisher Hippocrene.

Historic Black South by Joann Biondi and James Haskins publisher Hippocrene.

Museum Magazine Articles – 1992

"A Strong Sense of Mission," American Visions, Vol. 7, Number 1, Feb/March   1992 P.22.

"Seimert Park", American Visions, Vol. 7 Number 3, June July, 1992 P.26

Museum Magazine Articles - 1991

"Art of the African World: The Barnett-Aden Collection." Black Collegian 21:4   (March/April 1991): 40.

"Triumph Over Tragedy". American Visions, Vol. 6, Number 3, June 1991;   P.32.

Museum Magazine Articles - 1990

"Museum and Gallery Review." International Review of African-American Art   9:2 (1990: 48-49).

"An African-American Museum on the Mall." Pluralism or Ghettoization? Reconstruction 1:1 (Winter 1990: 41-48).

Museum Magazine Articles - 1989

Jefferson, Karen L. "Spotlight: Moorland - Springarn Research Center." American Visions 4:4 (August 1989): 46-47

Mohr, Nancy L. "Treasurer on an Island: the Penn Center on South Carolina's Sea Islands." American Visions 4:5 (October 1989): 29.

Holmes, Marian Smith. "The Quest for a Black Museum." American Visions 4:6 (December 1989): 44-49.

Museum Magazine Articles – 1988

"To Nova Scotia in Search of Liberty", American Visions, Vol. 3 Number 2, April 1988, P.22.

Marshall, Marilyn. "Black Fashions Past and Present: Harlem Museum, Showcases Attire From Slavery to Now." Ebony 63:7 (May 1988): 118-127.

"Dunbar: LA's Awakened Sleeping Beauty", American Visions, Vol. 3 Number 3, June 1988, P.25.

"Visiting Black History Treasures in the Nation's Capitol: Washington, D.C., has many famed Black Museums.: Ebony 63:8 (June 1988): 76-81.

"South Carolina State's Hidden Treasure; the I.P. Stanback Museum and Planetarium", Ebony 63:11 (September 1988): 82-87.

Museum - Articles - 1986

Museums on the move (Black Museums), "American Visions" 1:2 March - April, 1986, 24-34.

Museum Magazine Articles - 1983

"The Hatch-Billops Collection - Afro-American Cultural History", Dance Research Journal 15:2 Spring 1983 p.49.

"The Schoberg Library Then and Now", Freedomways, Vol. 23, No. 1 (1983), pp. 29-37.

Museum - Newspaper Articles

Chicago Tribune, Black History in Missouri, Sunday, June 2, 2002. Section 8 page16.

Chicago Tribune, Milwaukee Museum Documents Blacks' Struggle, Sunday, August 27, 2000, Section 8 page13.

Chicago Sun – Times, The West's Unsung Heroes, Sunday June 11, 1995.

Chicago Sun – Times, Music Fades on Dancer's Cultural Crusade, Chicago born Dunham Plagued by Sack of Funds, Sunday, August 13, 1995 page 19.

Chicago Sun – Times, Midwest Sites Salute African – Americans, Sunday, February 20, 1994.

Chicago Defender, A Hall of Their Own, Wednesday, July 6, 1994.

Chicago Tribune, Plan For Black Museums Brings Out The Old Rebel in Jesse Helms, Sunday, July 10, 1994 Section 2 page 2.

Citizen Newspaper Chicago, Two Extraordinary Grassroots Museums Dedicated To Educating Black America, Week of January 21, 1993.

Chicago Sun – Times, Sorrow and Celebration, Sunday, January 31, 1993 D. Page 4.

Chicago Sun – Times, Savvy Cities Tap Into Black Tourism, Sunday, February 7, 1993.

Chicago Tribune, DuSable Founder Blaze New Trails of Art, Culture, Wednesday, February 10, 1993, Black History Travel Section page 8.

Chicago Tribune, Rediscovery Black America, Sunday, February 14, 1993. Travel Section.

Chicago Sun – Times, Coast to Coast in Search of Black History, Sunday, February 14, 1993.

Chicago Sun – Times, Museum Launches Wing Prayer, Thursday, February 18, 1993.

Chicago Defender, Black History Preserved in Tennessee, Monday, March 1, 1993.page16.

Chicago Tribune, The Hit Factory, Sunday March 7, 1993 Travel Section.

Chicago Sun – Times, Past Comes Alive at Great Blacks In Was Museum, Sunday, April 4, 1993 D page3.

Chicago Citizen Newspaper Week, Two Notable Tennessee Attractions Preserve Black History, April 22, 1993 page28.

Chicago Sun – Times, The Black Frontier Fighters, Sunday, May 9, 1993.

Chicago Sun – Times, Collections Exhibit, Growing Interest in Black Memorabilia, Sunday, May 16, 1993.

Chicago Tribune, Power of the Past, Sunday, May 16, 1993.

Chicago Sun – Times, Black Fashion Museum Fills Void in United States History, Sunday, June 6, 1993 D page7.

Chicago Defender, Grant Provided for Civil Rights Library, Saturday, July 24, 1993.

Chicago Tribune Revised West, Sunday, July 25, 1993, Travel Section.

Chicago Sun – Times, Savoring the South's Black Heritage, Sunday, August 15, 1993, Travel Section.

Chicago Sun – Times, On the Blues Trail in the Mississippi Delta, Sunday, August 29, 1993.

Chicago Sun-Times, New Showcase for Black History? Sunday, July 5, 1992, p.16.

Chicago Sun-Times, Museums Court Black Staffers Audience, Friday, June 26, 1992.

Chicago Sun-Times, Museums Aim For A Larger Minority Audience, Sunday, June 7, 1992.

The Miami Times, "Heritage Museum Opens Branch In Space Donates By Owner of Liberty Flea Market", Thursday, June 4, 1992, 2C.

The Miami Times, "Heritage Museum Opens Branch In Space Donates By Owner of Liberty Flea Market," Thursday, June 4, 1992, 2c.

Chicago Defender, Civil Rights Museum and Justice, Saturday, June 22, 1991.

Chicago Defender, National African American Museum, Tuesday, May 7, 1991

Bibliographical Sources

Alabama Bureau of Tourism & Travel Black Heritage

Afro-American Alliance, Chicago, Illinois

African American Museum Association, Washington, D.C.

Afro-American Guide by Bertha Rhodes

American Association for State and Local History, Nashville, Tennessee

American Association of Museums, Washington, D.C.

Arkansas Tourist and Travel Bureau Black Heritage Experience

Baltimore Maryland African – American Heritage Visitors Guide Baltimore Area Convention and Visitors Association

Black Ethnic Collectibles Magazine

Black Resource Guide Book, 1983 Edition

Black Resource Guide 1988-89 Edition

149

California Department of Parks and Recreation Office of historic Preservation, Five Views on Ethnic Historic Site

Chicago Historical Society, Chicago, Illinois

Chicago Defender Newspaper, Chicago, Illinois

Chicago Historical Society, Chicago, Illinois

Columbus Georgia Black Heritage Guide Columbus Convention and Visitor s Bureau

Detroit Michigan Guide to African – American Points of Interest

DuSable Museum, Chicago, Illinois

Ebony Magazine, Chicago, Illinois

Essence Magazine, New York, New York

Florida Black Heritage Trail, Department of State, State of Florida

Georgia Tourist and Travel Bureau

Harold Washington Public Library, Chicago, Illinois

Illinois Tourist and Travel Bureau, African American Heritage Guide

Jacksonville, Florida Black Heritage Visitor Guide by the Beaches Convention and Visitors Bureau

Jekyll Island Black Heritage Guide Jekyll Island Convention and Visitors Bureau

Kansas City, Missouri Black Information Guide Convention and Visitors Bureau

Lorain County, Ohio, African – American Heritage Tour Lorain County Visitor's Bureau

Louisiana Tourist and Travel Bureau

Macon, Georgia Black Heritage Guide

Maryland Tourist and Travel Bureau African – American Culture

Miami Visitor's Guide to Black Miami in the State of Florida by Miami – Dade Chamber of Commerce

Michigan Tourist Bureau

Mississippi Department of Economic and Community Development - Division of Tourism Development

Missouri's African – American Heritage by Missouri State Travel and Tourism Bureau

Negro Almanac Edition 1983

New England, A Culture Guide to African – American Heritage, by Linda Cline and Robert C. Hayden

New Orleans Louisiana Black Heritage of New Orleans in the State of Louisiana By Greater New Orleans Tourist and Convention Commission and Greater New Orleans Black Tourism Network of New Orleans

Ohio Division of Travel and Tourism Bureau, Ohio Cross Cultural Adventure Guide

Oklahoma African – American History, Attractions and Events, Oklahoma Tourism And Recreation Department

Pennsylvania Tourist Bureau

Savannah African – American Heritage Savannah Convention and Bureau

South Carolina Department of Parks, Recreation and Tourism

To Walk the Whole: African – American Cultural Resources in South Carolina by Department of Parks, Recreation and Tourism

St. Louis, Missouri Convention and Visitors Commission

Tennessee Tourism Development, the Roots of Tennessee an African - American Guide

Virginia Tourism, Pathways to African – American Heritage

Vision Magazine, Washington, D.C.

Visitors Guide to Black Milwaukee, Wisconsin

Washington, D. C. Black History National Recreation Trail in The District of Columbia by National Park Service

INDEX

A

ABIBIMAN TREASUR OF BLACK ARTS MUSEUM, 28
ABOLITIONISTS, 58, 79
ACCRA, GHANA, 71
ADAMS, JOHN QUINCY, 76
ADDERLEY, CANNONBALL COLLECTION, 63
AFRICA, XIII, 3, 4, 52, 59, 60, 72, 76, 79, 84, 86, 92, 93, 97, 102, 106, 135, 142
AFRICA FACT SHEET, 142
AFRICAN-AMERICAN ARCHITECTS AND ARCHITECTURE, 50
AFRICAN-AMERICAN CULTURAL AND GENEALOGICAL SOCIETY OF ILLINOIS MUSEUM, 22
AFRICAN-AMERICAN CULTURAL AND HISTORICAL SOCIETY MUSEUM, 92
AFRICAN-AMERICAN CULTURAL AND HISTORICAL MUSEUM, 28, 36
AFRICAN-AMERICAN FAMILY HISTORY ASSN., INC., 19
AFRICAN-AMERICAN FILM ORGANIZATIONS, 123
AFRICAN-AMERICAN FIREFIGHTER MUSEUM, 13, 52, 53
AFRICAN-AMERICAN HALL OF FAME MUSEUM, 28
AFRICAN-AMERICAN HERITAGE AND BLACK VETERANS ARCHIVES, 21
AFRICAN-AMERICAN HERITAGE CENTER, 23
AFRICAN-AMERICAN HERITAGE MUSEUM, 41, 104
AFRICAN-AMERICAN LIBRARIES, 119
AFRICAN-AMERICAN MUSEUM, 13, 42,124
AFRICAN-AMERICAN MUSEUM AND CULTURAL CENTER OF WESTERN MASSACHUSETTS, 27
AFRICAN-AMERICAN MUSEUM ASSOCIATION, 5, 114
AFRICAN-AMERICAN MUSEUM OF FINE ARTS, 14
AFRICAN-AMERICAN MUSEUM OF NASSAU COUNTY, 33
AFRICAN-AMERICAN MUSEUM OF THE ART, 17
AFRICAN-AMERICAN MUSEUMS IN CANADA, 44
AFRICAN-AMERICAN SUBJECT RELATED MUSEUMS, 129
AFRICAN-AMERICAN WAX AND HISTORY MUSEUM, 33
AFRICAN ART MUSEUM OF MARYLAND, 26
AFRICAN-CANADIAN, XII, XIII
AFRICAN HERITAGE STUDIES ASSOCIATION, 116
AFRICAN MEETING HOUSE, 27
AFRICAN MEETING HOUSE IN NANATUCKET, 27
AFRICAN PROVERB, 139
AFRICAN STUDIES AND RESEARCH PROGRAM, 15
AFRICAN STUDIES ASSOCIATION, 116
AFRICANA STUDIES AND RESEARCH CENTER, 117
AFRO-AMERICAN CULTURAL AND HISTORICAL SOCIETY MUSEUM, 112
AFRO-AMERICAN CULTURAL CENTER, 28, 35, 36, 90, 119
AFRO-AMERICAN CULTURAL FOUNDATION, 119
AFRO-AMERICAN CULTURAL HERITAGE CENTER, 40
AFRO-AMERICAN DOLL GALLERY, 15
AFRO-AMERICAN GENEAOLOGY AND HISTORICAL SOCIETY, 111
AFRO-AMERICAN HERITAGE ASSOCIAITON, 115

AFRO-AMERICAN HERITAGE MUSEUM, 26
AFRO-AMERICAN HISTORICAL AND CULTURAL MUSEUM, 85 94, 95
AFRO-AMERICAN HISTORICAL AND CULTURAL SOCIETY OF JERSEY CITY, 32, 111
AFRO-AMERICAN HISTORICAL AND GENEALOGICAL SOCIETY, INC., 112, 117
AFRO-AMERICAN HISTORICAL SOCIETY, 23, 111
AFRO-AMERICAN HISTORICAL SOCIETY OF DELAWARE, 15, 111
AFRO-AMERICAN HISTORICAL SOCIETY OF THE NIAGARA FRONTIER, 32, 111
AFRO-AMERICAN IN NEW YORK LIFE AND HISTORY, 116
AFRO-AMERICAN MANUSCRIPT COLLECTIONS, 131
AFRO-AMERICAN MUSIC BICENTENNIAL HALL OF FAME AND MUSEUM, INC., 37
AKRON, OHIO, 36, 141
AKWAA HARRISON GALLERY, 44
ALABAMA, 6, 11, 12, 49, 50, 51, 114, 119, 141
ALABAMA A AND M UNIVERSITY, 50
ALABAMA JAZZ HALL OF FAME MUSEUM, 11
ALABAMA STATE BLACK ARCHIVES RESEARCH CENTER AND MUSEUM, 11
ALAMANCE, NORTH CAROLINA, 100
ALASKA, 141
ALBANY, GEORGIA, 19
ALBANY CIVIL RIGHTS MOVEMENT MUSEUM AT OLD MT. ZION CHURCH, 19
ALBUQUERQUE, NEW MEXICO, 141
ALCORN, MISSISSIPPI, 141
ALEXANDER, EGYPT, 3
ALEXANDER, LOIS, K., 33, 57
ALEXANDRIA BLACK HISTORY, 106
ALEXANDRIA, LOUISIANA, 24
ALEXANDRIA RESOURCE CENTER, 106
ALEXANDRIA, VIRGINIA, 41, 106
ALFONSO, ARTHUR, 88
ALFORD, DECKER, MAE, 75
ALI, MUHAMMAD, 82
ALLEN, CAROLINE J, 17
ALLENSWORTH CALIFORNIA, 13
ALTON, ILLINOIS, 114
AMERICA'S BLACK HOLOCAUST MUSEUM (ABHM), 43
AMERICAN ASSOCIATION FOR STATE LOCAL HISTORY, 3
AMERICAN ASSOCIATION OF MUSEUMS, 3,5
AMERICAN COLONIZATION SOCIETY, 131
AMERICAN FRIENDS SERVICE COMMITTEE, 131
AMERICAN MISSIONARY ASSOCIATION, 67, 76, 89
AMERICAN NEGRO ACADEMY, 88
AMERICAN REVOLUTARY WAR, 73
AMHERSTRURG, 44
AMISTAD COMMITTEE, 76
AMISTAD FOUNDATION, 130
AMISTAD RESEARCH CENTER, 75
AMISTAD RESEARCH CENTER LIBRARY ARCHIVES, 24
ANACOSTA, 58
ANACOSTA MUSEUM, 56

ANACOSTIA MUSEUM SMITHSONIAN INSTITUTION, 16, 56
ANCHORAGE, ALASKA, 141
ANCIENT EGYPTIAN MUSEUM AND INSTITUTE, 21
ANDERSON, ELMER, 29, 82
ANGELOU, MAYA, 83
ANN ARBOR, MICHIGAN, 28
ANNAPOLIS, MARYLAND, 100
ANTELOPE VALLEY AFRICAN-AMERICAN MUSEUM, 13
ANTHROPOLOGISTS, 4
ANTIGUA GALLERY, INC., 18
APEX MUSEUM, 64
APEX AFRO- COLLETION OF LIFE AND HERITAGE, INC.,19
APPALACHIAN WHITES, 76
ARAWAKAN INDIANAS, 72
ARCHAEOLOGISTS, 4
ARCHDIOCESE OF WASHINGTON OFFICE OF BLACK CATHOLICS, 115
ARMSTRONG'S HOUSE AND ARCHIVES, 34
ARIZONA, 12, 112, 141
ARIZONA CHAPTER AAHG, 112
ARKANSAS, 12, 13, 51
ARNOLD, MARYLAND, 118
ARMSTRONG, LOUIS HOUSE, 87
ARMSTRONG, LUCILLE, 87
ART, 3, 6
ART CONSORTIUM AFRICAN-AMERICAN MUSEUM UNION TERMINAL, 36
ART DECO, 83
ART'N ARTIFACTS GALLERY, 20
ART INSTITUTE OF CHICAGO, 73
ASH GROVE, MISSOURI, 30
ASHVILLE, NORTH CAROLINA, 35, 90
ASIA, 71, 76
ASSOCIATION FOR THE STUDY OF AFRO-AMERICAN LIFE AND HISTORY, 114
ASSOCIATION FOR THE STUDY OF ANCIENT AFRICAN CIVILIZAITONS, 116
ASSOCIATION FOR THE STUDY OF BLACK LIFE AND HISTORY, 72, 73
ASSOCIATION FOR THE STUDY OF CLASSICAL AFRICAN CIVILIZATION, 115
ASSOCIATION FOR THE STUDY OF NEGRO LIFE AND HISTORY, 143
ASSOCIATION OF AFRICAN HISTORIANS, 116
ASSOCIIATIONS, 118
ASTRONOMY, 97
ATKINS, TEXAS, 40
ATLANTA CONSTITUTION, NEWSPAPER, VI
ATLANTA COSTAL PLAIN, 97
ATLANTA FULTON PUBLIC LIBRARY, 120
ATLANTA GEORGIA,19, 20, 64, 65, 114, 116, 117, 120, 122
ATLANTA LIFE INSURANCE COMPANY, 65
ATLANTA UNIVERISTY, 65, 67, 76
ATTUCKS, CRISPUS HIGH SCHOOL MUSEUM, 74
ATTUCKS, CRISPUS MUSEUM, 23
AUNT ESTHER, 129

AUNT LEN'S DOLL AND TOY MUSEUM, 33
AURORA, ILLINOIS, 21
AUSTIN, GEORGIA, 20
AUSTIN, TEXAS 102, 103
AVERY INSTITUE RESEARCH CENTER FOR AFRO-AMERICAN HISTORY AND CULTURE, 97, 98
AVIATION, 6

B

BAILEY, JOYCE, 15
BAKER, CHRISTINE, 79
BALCH INSTITUTE FOR ETHNIC STUDIES, 131
BALDWIN COUNTY, 67
BALTIMORE CHAPTER AAHGS, 113
BALTIMORE, MARYLAND, 58, 76, 113, 120
BALL, THOMAS, 130
BALLARD OF CASEY JONES, 137
BAMBAHA, 135
BANKERS TRUST COMPANY, 88
BATTLE, THOMAS C., 16
BARAKA, AMIRI, 86
BARNETT-ADEN COLLECTION, 56
BARTOW ELEMENTARY SCHOOL, 65
BASEBALL, 74
BAY, EDNA DR., 116
BEACH INSTITUTE, 67
BEACON HILL, 78
BEALE STREET BLUES, 49
BEATTY, TALLEY, 86
BEAUX ARTS CLASSICAL, 65
BECK CULTURAL EXCHANGE CENTER, 39, 100
BECK, ETHEL, 100
BECK, ETHEL HOME FOR ORPHANS, 99
BECK, JAMES, 100
BEECHER, LYMAN, 136
BELLSOUTH, 64
BELSON, JERRY, 12
BENNEHAN-CAMERION FAMILY, 135
BENSON, CLAY, 42
BENTON HARBOR, MICHIGAN, 28
BEREA COLLEGE, 76, 142
BERNITA, ASSA TOUR, 14
BERUNI RA `SHUAL OHMA, 75, 91
BETHUNE-COOKMAN COLLEGE, 59
BETHUNE MUSEUM AND ARCHIVES, INC., 16, 57, 60
BIAFADA, 135
BICKFORD, STEPHEN, 134
BILOXI, MISSISSIPPI, 102

BIRMINGHAM, ALABAMA, 11, 119
BIRMINGHAM CIVIL RIGHTS INSTITUTE, 11
BIRMINGHAM PUBLIC AND JEFFERSON COUNTY FREE LIBRARY, 119
BIRTH OF A NATION, 143
BISHOP COLLEGE, 103
BISHOP STATE BLACK HISTORY MUSEUM, 11
BLACK AMERICAN CINEMA SOCIETY, 124
BLACK AMERICAN WEST MUSEUM AND HERITAGE CENTER, 14, 54
BLACK AMERICANS IN CONGRESS, 63
BLACK ARCHIVES HISTORY AND RESEARCH FOUNDATION, 18
BLACK ARCHIVES HISTORY AND RESEARCH FOUNDATION OF SOUTH FLORIDA, 62
BLACK ARCHIVES OF MID-AMERICA, 31
BLACK ARCHIVES RESEARCH CENTER MUSEUM, 63
BLACK ARTS NATIONAL DIASPORA MUSEUM, 24
BLACK CATHOLIC HISTORY RESOURCE CENTER, 115
BLACK CINEMA GALLERY, 81
BLACK CIVIL WAR TRIBUNE COMMITTEE, 115
BLACK COWBOYS, 55
BLACK CULTURAL CENTER FOR NOVA SCOTIA, 45
BLACK EDUCATION AND CULTURAL HISTORY, INC., 115
BLACK FANEUIL HALL, 78
BLACK FASHION MUSEUM, 6, 15, 57, 88
BLACK FASHION MUSEUM HARLEM INSTITUTE OF FASHION, 33
BLACK FILM CENTER/ARCHIVE, 123
BLACK FILM INSTITUTE, 124
BLACK FILM MAKERS FOUNDATION, 124
BLACK HERITAGE GALLERY, 41
BLACK HERITAGE MUSEUM, 18, 63
BLACK HERITAGE SOCIETY OF WASHINGTON STATE, INC., 42, 112
BLACK HERITAGE TOURS, 114
BLACK HERITAGE TRAIL TOURS, 114
BLACK HISTORICAL ARTS MUSEUM, 11
BLACK HISTORY ARCHIVES, 91
BLACK HISTORY EXHIBIT CENTER, 119
BLACK HISTORY MUSEUM AND CULTURAL CENTER, INC., 42
BLACK HOLOCAUST MUSEUM, 28
BLACK INVENTIONS MUSEUM, 124
BLACK JOCKEY, 134
BLACK KANSAS ARCHIVES, 75
BLACK LEGENDS OF PROFESSIONAL BASKETBALL, 28
BLACK MEMORABILIA, 117
BLACK MILITARY HISTORY, 118
BLACK MILITARY HISTORY INSTITUTE OF AMERICA, INC., 118
BLACK MILITARY HISTORY SOCIETY, 118
BLACK PRESS ARCHIVES, 59
BLACK REVOLUTIONARY WAR PATRIOTS FOUNDATION, 115
BLACK STUDIES AND LIBRARY ASSOCIAITON OF FINDLAY AND HANCOCK COUNTIES, 36, 93
BLACK TEXAN'S HALL OF FAME, 40, 103
BLACK TOWNS, 5, 54

BLACK WOMEN AGAINST THE ODDS, 50
BLACK WORLD HISTORY MUSEUM, 31
BLAIR-CALDWELL AFRICAN-AMERICAN RESEARCH LIBRARY, 120
BLOOMINGTON, INDIANA, 111, 123
BLOOMINGTON - NORMAL BLACK HISTORY PROJECT, 114
BLUES HERITAGE, 133
BLY, SIMON JR., 119
BMCA (BLACK MEMORABILIA COLLECTION'S ASSOCIATION), 118
BOISE, IDAHO, 21, 69
BOISE PRESBYTERIAN CHURCH, 69
BOKARI, 91
BOKONGO, 135
BOLEY, OKLAHOMA, 141
BOND, JULIAN, 63, 82
BONTEMPS, ARNA AFRICAN-AMERICAN AND CULTURAL CENTER, 24
BOOKS, 6
BOOKER, FANNIE, 30
BOOKER, KENNETH, 39
BOSTON, MASSACHUSETTS, 27, 78
BOSS, MARTIN, 66
BOWLING, ALLEN LAFAYETTE, 82
BOWN, PATTI, 86
BOX, ANNA, VI
BOX, WILLIE, SR., VI.
BOYD, RUBY, 37
BRACY, ALECIA, 35
BRADENTON, FLORIDA, 17
BRADY, MATTHEW, 130
BRAND, CABELL, 105
BRANDON, MAX, 81
BRAZIL, 79
BREEDING ROOM, 135
BREWSTER OLD TIMERS, 82
BRIDGES, ANNETTE, 31
BRIER, RABBIT, , 129
BRIGHAM YOUNG, UTAH, 69
BRIGHT, OSBOURN W., 89
BRIGADE, ABRAHAM LINCOLN, 73
BROACH, BARBARA, 11
BROCKMAN GALLERY, 13
BRONX, NEW YORK, 118
BRONZEVILLE CHILDREN'S MUSEUM, 21
BROOKLYN, DODGERS, 84
BROOKLYN NEW YORK, 32, 85, 113
BROWARD COUNTY, 61
BROWN CHARLOTTE HAWKINS HISTORICAL FOUNDATION, INC., 35, 89
BROWN COUNTY, 136
BROWN, MAJOR C. Rev., 122
BROWN, MAUREEN, 118

BROWN, MORRIS COLLEGE, 20
BROWN, SCOTLAND C., 21
BROWN V. THE BOARD OF EDUCATIN, 6
BRUNSON, THEODORE, 85
BRUNSON, THEODORE, 32
BRUNSWICK, ELIZABETH, 67
BRUNSWICK, MAINE, 129
BRURROUGHS, CHARLES, 73
BRYANT, HAZEL, 86
BRYANT, LINDA, 34
BRYANT, NORMAN, 29, 81
BUBBLING BROWN SUGAR, 88
BUFFALO, NEW YORK, 32, 111 116
BUFFALO, SOLDIER, 50, 75
BUFFALO SOLDIERS NATIONAL MUSEUM, 41
BUFORD, ELLINGTON, 98
BUMSTEAD, NORRIS, 65
BUNCHE, RALPH J. ORAL HISTORY COLLECTION, 59
BUREAU OF PUBLICITY AND INFORMATION, 114
BURGESS, 5
BURKLE ESTATE, 137
BURROUGHS, MARGARET, 73
BURTON, BRENT, 13
BUXTON NATIONAL HISTORIC SITE AND MUSEUM, 44

C

CADBY, PAUL DR., 63
CALEB, JOSEPH COMMUNITY CENTER, 18
CALIFORNIA, 13, 14, 51 - 54, 112, 115 – 118, 124, 141
CALIFORNIA, AFRICAN-AMERICAN GENEALOGY SOCIETY, 112
CALIFORNIA AFRO-AMERICAN MUSEUM, 13, 51, 52
CALLOWAY, BERTHA, 31
CAMERON, JAMES, 43
CAMMBRIDGE, MARYLAND, 26, 76, 115
CAMPBELL, EMORY, 39
CANADA, 133, 136
CANARY COTTAGE, 89
CANNONBALL, 137
CANTON, MISSISSIPPI, 137
CARNEGIE LIBRARY, 94
CAPITOL HILL, 100
CARBONDALE, ILLINOIS, 112
CARIBBEAN, 52, 72, 77, 84, 93, 97
CARNEGIE PUBLIC LIBRARY BOARD OF TRUSTEES, 133
CARRINGTON, GLENN COLLECTION, 59
CARTER'S GROVE PLANTATION, 132
CARTERSVILLE, GEORGIA, 20

CARVER COMMUNITY CULTURAL CENTER, 41
CARVER, GEORGE WASHINGTON, 6
CARVER, GEORGE WASHINGTON MUSEUM, 102
CARVER, GEORGE WASHINGTON MUSEUM AND CULTURAL CENTER, 12
CARVER, GEORGE WASHINGTON MUSEUM/PUBLIC LIBRARY, 40
CARVER HILL MEMORIAL MUSEUM FAIRVIEW PARK, 17
CARVER HILL MUSEUM, 61
CASH, WILLIAM, 95
CASSVILLE, GEORGIA, 65, 66
CATHOLIC NUN, 79
CEDAR HILL, 58
CEMI, 72
CENTRAL AFRICA, 4
CENTRAL AMERICA, 104
CENTRAL CITY COMPLEX, 99
CENTRAL EVENING HIGH SCHOOL, 88
CENTRAL FLORIDA CHAPTER AAHG, 112
CENTER FOR BLACK HISTORY, ART AND FOLKLORE, 96
CENTRAL MARYLAND CHAPTER AAHG'S, 113
CENTRAL PENNSYLVANIA AFRICAN-AMERICAN MUSEUM, 38
CERAMIC, 6
CHAMPAIGN, ILLINOIS, 21
CHANDLER, KAREN, 38
CHAPMAN, DOROTHY, 101
CHAPMAN HOUSE MUSEUM, 18, 62
CHAPMAN, WILLIAM A., SR., DR., 62
CHARLESTON, SOUTH CAROLINA, 38, 96, 97
CHARLESTON, WEST VIRGINIA, 141
CHARLOTTE-MEKLENBURG AFRO-AMERICAN CULTURAL SERVICE CENTER, 35
CHARLOTTE, NORTH CAROLINA, 35, 90
CHATTANOOGA, TENNESSEE, 39, 98, 99
CHATTANOOGA AFRICAN-AMERICAN HERITAGE COUNCIL, 99
CHATTANOOGA AFRICAN-AMERICAN MUSEUM, 99
CHATTONOOGA AFRICAN-AMERICAN MUSEUM AND RESEARCH CENTER, 39
CHATTONOOGA AREA LITERACY MOVEMENT, 98
CHEASAPEAKE COUNTY, 132
CHESS RECORDS MUSEUM, 21
CHIANG, FAY, 86
CHICAGO, ILLINOIS, 5, 21, 22, 69 – 74, 111 – 113, 116, 120
CHICAGO PARK DISTRICT, 73
CHICAGO WORLD FAIR, 49
CHICANOS, 76
CHICKEN GEORGE,M , 100
CHIN CHARLIE, 86
CHRISTIANITY, 72
CHURCH CREEK, MARYLAND, 77
CICERO, 7
CINCINNATI, OHIO, 36, 129, 133
CINQUE, 76

CITY COLLEGES OF CHICAGO, 70
CIVIL RIGHTS MOVEMENT, 103
CIVIL WAR, 56, 75, 78, 97, 107, 137
CLARKSDALE COUNTY, 133
CLARKSDALE, MISSISSIPPI, 133
CLAYTON, ALONZO, 134
CLEARWATER, FLORIDA, 17
CLEVELAND, OHIO, 36, 91, 92, 112, 113, 120
CLOTH, 6
COAHOMA COUNTY, 133
COCONUT GROVE, 62
COFFIN, CATHERINE, 133
COFFIN LEVI STATE HISTORIC SITE, 133
COFFIN, LEWIS, 133
COLORED, 142
COLE, ALLEN E., 91
COLLEGE OF CHARLESTON, 98
COLEMAN, KIMETHA, 21
COLLEGE, 7
COLONEL ALLEN ALLENSWORTH STATE HISTORIC PARK, 13
COLONIAL WILLIAMSBURG'S HISTORIC AREA, 132
COLORADO, 14, 54, 55, 120
COLTRANE, JOHN W. HOUSE AND SOCIETY, 37
COLUMBIA, MARYLAND, 26, 113
COLUMBIA, SOUTH CAROLINA, 38, 96
COLUMBUS, GEORGIA, 20, 141
COLUMBUS, OHIO, 141
COMMODORES MUSEUM, 12
COMMUNITY FOLK ART GALLERY, 34
COMMUNITY FOR AFRO-AMERICAN HISTORY OBSERVANCES, 116
COMMUNITY ON BLACK PIONEERS ALTON MUSEUM, 114
COMPTON, CALIFORNIA, 141
CONCEPT EAST, II, 81
CONGO REPUBLIC, 71
CONGRESS, 56, 58, 102
CONGRESSIONAL, 101
CONNECTICUT, 15, 55, 111, 130, 141
CONNECTICUT AFRO-AMERICAN HISTORICAL SOCIETY, INC., 15, 55, 56, 111
CONSOLIDATED BANK AND TRUST, 106
CONSTITUTION, 6
COOK, DERRICK, 16
COOK, LOUISE, 19
COOK, STEVEN, 45
COOKSTOVE CHEMIST, 103
COON, 63
CORAL GABLES, FLORIDA, 62
CORONA, NEW YORK, 87
COSTUMES, 6
COTTAGE MUSEUM, VI

COURT HOUSE, XII
COURTNEY, VERNON, 36
COVINGTON, KENTUCKY, 141
COWANS, THELMA, 82
COWBOYS, 5, 55
CRANE JUNIOR COLLEGE, 70
CRENSHAW HOUSE, 134
CRENSHAWM, JOHN HART, 134, 135
CRESTVIEW, FLORIDA, 17, 61
CRIPPENS, DAVID, 13
CROW, JIM, 61
CRUMP, MR., 49
CULLEN, COUNTEE, 88,
CULLEN, COUNTREE BRANCH LIBRARY, 121
CULTURAL MONUMENT #289, 53
CUMMINGS, ROBERT DR., 15

D

DADE COUNTY, 62
DARLINGTON, SOUTH CAROLINA, 38
DARLINGTON CULTURAL REALISM CHARM, 38
DALLAS, TEXAS, 40, 103
DAR ES SALAAM, 71, 72
DARTMOUTH, CANADA, 45
DAVIS, ALONZO, 13
DAVIS, BELLAH MYRTLE, 76
DAVIS, CALEB, A., 18
DAVIS, E. BEN, 82
DAVIS HARDING, ELISE, 44
DAVIS, JULIA COLLECTION, 121
DAVIS, OSSIE, 83
DAVIS, PAT, 34
DAVIS, RUSSELL, 92
DAVIS, SALLIE ELLIS HOUSE, 67
DAVIS, ULYSSESS COLLECTION, 67
DAWSON, CHARLES, 72
DAYTON, OHIO, 36, 92
DAYTONA BEACH, FLORIDA, 17
DECATUR, ILLINOIS, 22
DECLARATION OF INDEPENDENCE, 6
DEE, RUBY, 83
DELAND FLORIDA, 17
DELAWARE, 15, 111, 141
DELTA BLUES MUSEUM,.133
DELTONA, FLORIDA, 112
DENVER, COLORADO, 14, 54, 55, 120
DESHIELDS, WILLIAM A. COL., 118

DES MOINES, IOWA, 141
DETROIT, MICHIGAN, 28, 79 – 82, 113, 120, 122
DETROIT PUBLIC LIBRARY, 121
DILLARD UNIVERSITY, 75
DISTRICT OF COLUMBIA, 15, 56 – 60, 112, 114, 115, 117, 118, 120, 143
DISTRICT OF COLUMBIA PUBLIC LIBRARY, 120
DOCTOR, 55
DODSON, EDITH, 86
DODSON, HOWARD, 34
DODSON, OWEN, 86
DOLEMAN, MARQUENTE, 26
DOLEMAN, MARQUENTE HOUSE MUSEUM, 77
DOLLS, 6, 95
DOMINICAN REPUBLIC, 72
DONALDSONVILLE, LOUISIANA, 24
DORCHESTER COUNTY, 77
DOUGLAS HIGH SCHOOL, 142
DOUGLASS, FREDERICK, 78, 143
DOUGLASS, FREDERICK HOME, 16
DOUGLASS, FREDERICK, MEMORIAL AND HISTORICAL ASSOCIATION, 118
DOUGLASS, FREDERICK MUSEUM AND CULTRUAL CENTER, 34
DOUGLASS, FREDERICK NATIONAL HISTORICAL SITE, 58
DOUGLASS-TRUTH LIBRARY, 122
DOVER, DELAWARE, 141
DOWNSTATE AFRO-AMERICAN HALL OF FAME MUSEUM, 22
DRAPER, ELIZABETH, 107
DRED SCOTT V. SANFORD, 6
DRESDEN, CANADA, 45
DUBOIS, W.E.B., 5, 67, 88
DUES, LEROY, 82
DUNBAR HOTEL CULTURAL AND HISTORICAL MUSEUM, 14
DUNBAR HOUSE, 92
DUNBAR, MATILDA, 92, 93
DUNBAR, PAUL LAWRENCE, 92, 131
DUNBAR, PAUL LAWRENCE HOUSE STATE MEMORIAL, 36
DUNHAM, KATHERINE MUSEUM, 22
DUNNAWAY, VIRGINIA, 85
DUNNING, 5
DUNMORE, PENNSYLVANNIA, 131
DURHAM, NORTH CAROLINA, 35, 135
DUSABLE, JEAN BAPTISTE POINTE, 5
DUSABLE MUSEUM, 111
DUSABLE MUSEUM OF AFRICAN-AMERICAN HISTORY, 22, 72, 73, 74,
DUTRIEULLIE, ALBERT E., 131

E

EAST BAY NEGRO HISTORICAL SOCIETY, 14, 53
EAST CLEVELAND, OHIO, 141
EAST ST. LOUIS, ILLINOIS, 22
EATON, GEORGIA, 129
EATON, JAMES, 18
EATONVILLE, FLORIDA, 17, 62
EBONY MUSEUM OF ART, 14
EBONY MUSEUM OF NEGRO HISTORY, 73
EDAW, EUGENE, 72
EDDY SCHOOL, 67
EDEN, NORTH CAROLINA, 35
EDMONDS, S. RANDOLPH, 63
EDUCATION OF THE NEGRO PRIOR TO 1861, 143
EDWARDS, ESTHER, 80
EGYPTIAN HISTORICAL SOCIETY, 111
ELEMENTARY SCHOOL, 7
ELDRIDGE, RAY, 86
ELIOT, CHARLES, 89
ELIZA, 129, 133
ELLICOTT CITY, MARYLAND, 26
ELLIS, JOSH, 67
ELMORE COUNTY BLACK HISTORY MUSEUM, 50, 51
ELMORE COUNTY ASSOCIATION OF BLACK HERITAGE MUSEUM OF BLACK HISTORY, 12
ELMORE, GWENDOLYN, 24
EMANCIPATION PROCLAMATION, 6, 100
EMOBA THE MUSEUM OF BLACK ARKANSANS, 12
EMORY UNIVERSITY, 116
ENGINE NO. 382, 137
ENOCH PRATT FREE LIBRARY, 120
EQUALITY, ILLINOIS, 134
EQUIPMENT, 6
ETCHINGS, 6
ETHIOPIA, 4, 63, 71, 142
ETHNIC HERITAGE CHILDREN'S MUSUEM, 62
ETHNIC MINORITIES MEMORABILIA ASSOCIATION, 13
EUBIE, 88
EUROPE, 59, 72, 103, 131
EUROPEAN LAW, XII
EVANS TIBBS COLLECTION, 58
EVANSVILLE, INDIANA, 22
EVANSVILLE AFRICAN-AMERICAN MUSEUMS, 22
EVERS, MEDGER MUSEUM, 30
EWERT, BERN, 105
EXODUSTERS AWARNESS, INC., 116

F

FAIRBANKS, ALASKA, 141
FARISH STREET HISTORIC DISTRICT, 83
FATHER OF BLUES, 49
FAYETTE, ALABAMA, 83
FAYETTEVILLE, NORTH CAROLINA, 141
FELDMAN, EUGENE, 73
FIELD MUSEUM, 70
FIELDS, VILMA SCRUGGS, 39
FINDLAY, OHIO, 36
FINNEY ART, 82
FINNEY, THEODORE, 80
FIRST AFRICAN BAPTIST CHURCH, 68
FIRST NATIONAL BLACK HISTORICAL SOCIETY OF KANSAS, 23, 75
FISK UNIVERSITY, 69, 76, 88
FISK UNIVERSITY MUSEUM OF ART, 40
FLANKLIN, JACK, 94
FLEMING, THOMAS, 92
FLEWELLEN, ICABOD, 92
FINDLAY, OHIO, 93, 94
FLINT, MICHIGAN, 29
FLINT MUSEUM OF AFRICAN-AMERICAN HISTORY, 29
FLORENCE, ALABAMA, 1, 49
FLORIDA, 17, 18, 19, 61, 97, 112, 120, 141
FLORIDA A & M UNIVERSITY, 63
FLORIDA LEGISTATURE, 62, 63
FLUSHING, NEW YORK, 116
FOLK DOLLS, 95
FORDHAM, MONROE DR., 32
FORD, JUSTINA DR., 55
FORESTVILLE, MARYLAND, 112
FORT CONCHO, 129
FORT DEL MOSE, FLORIDA, 5
FORT LAUDERDALE, FLORIDA, 17 61
FORT LEVENWORTH, KANSAS, 111
FORT MEADE, MARYLAND, 118
FORT MOSE, 62
FORT STANTON PARK, 56
FORT WAYNE, INDIANA, 141
FORT WORTH PUBLIC LIBRARY, 122
FORT WORTH, TEXAS, 41,112, 113
FORTY ACRES AND A MULE, INC., 122,123
FORTY-MINERS, 53
FOSSILS, 4
FOSTER, RUBE, 85
FOSTER, STEPHEN STATE FOLK CULTURAL CENTER, 19
FOUNTAIN CITY, INDIANA, 133

FRALIN AND WALDRON, 104
FRALIN, HORACE, 105
FRANKFORT, KENTUCKY, 141
FRANKLIN, JACK, 94
FRANKLIN, KENTUCKY, 22
FREE LIBRARY OF PHLADELPHIA, 122
FREEMEN'S BUREAU, 67
FREETOWN VILLAGE, 122
FRENCH BENJAMIN COLLECTION, 63
FRENCH BLACK BISQUE DOLLS, 95
FRESNO, CALIFORNIA, 13
FRIENDS OF BLACK HISTORY, 106
FUGITIVE SLAVE LAW OF 1850, 133 , 136
FUR TRADE, 54, 55, 73

G

GADSDEN, ALABAMA, 11
GAIL LAUREN INFORMATION, 63
GAITHER, EDMUND BARRY, 27
GAITHER, JAKE, 64
GALLERY OF ART, 16
GALLOWAY, ROBERT DR., 41
GAME COCK TRAINER, 100
GARDENA, CALIFORNIA, 117
GARVEY, MARCUS, 104
GARY, INDIANA, 141
GEE, SAMUEL, 82
GENEALOGICAL SOCIETIES, 112
GENEALOGY, 75
GENESIS II MUSEUM OF INTERNATIONAL BLACK CULTURE, 33
GEORGETOWN, SOUTH CAROLINA, 116
GEORGIA, 19, 20, 21, 64-68, 100, 114, 116, 117, 120, 122, 129, 137
GEORGIA DEPARTMENT OF INDUSTRY AND TRADE, 114
GEORGIA JOURNAL, 68
GEORGIA STATE INDUSTRIAL COLLEGE, 68
GERMAN, 102
GERMAN BLACK BISQUE DOLLS, 95
GHANA, 71
GIBSON, ALTHEA, 82
GILBERT, RALPH MARK CIVIL RIGHTS MUSEUM, 6, 21, 68
GILLESPIE, DIZZY, 86
GLASS, 6
GOLDEN GATE LIBRARY, 53
GOLD RUSH, 53
GOROY, BARRY, 80
GOSPEL MUSIC HALL OF FAME AND MUSEUM, 28
GRANT, MICKI, 86

GRAYSTONE INTERNATIONAL JAZZ MUSEUM, 28, 79, 80
GREAT PLAINS BLACK MUSEUM, 31
GREATER FLINT AFRO-AMERICAN HALL OF FAME, 29, 81, 82
GREENSBORO, NORTH CAROLINA, 35, 89
GREENVILLE PUBLIC LIBRARY, 85
GRIFFITH, JOHN, 73
GRINNELL GALLERY, 34
GROVEY V. TOWNSEND, 6
GUINEA COST, 60
GUINN V. UNITED STATES, 6

H

HACKLEY, AZALIA MEMORIAC COLLECTION, 121
HADAR, 4
HAGERSTOWN, MARYLAND, 26, 77
HAITI, 58, 72, 93
HALEY, ALEX STATE HISTORIC STIE AND MUSEUM, 39, 100
HALFADRE, FRANK E., 37
HALIBURTON, MARYANN, 37
HALL, BOOKER T., 36
HAMLORICK, KATHE, 24
HAMMOND'S HOUSE, 20
HAMPTON, VIRGINIA, 42
HAMPTON UNIVERSITY, 76, 105
HAMPTON UNIVERSITY MUSEUM, 42
HANDY, W. C. CABIN MUSEUM, 6, 11, 49
HANDY, WILLIAM CHRISTOPHER, 49, 133
HARLEM INSTITUTE OF FASHION, 88
HARLEM RENAISSANCE, 52, 56, 62
HARMON, JOHN, 35
HARPER, MARY, 90
HARRISBURG, PENNSYLVANIA, 141
HARRIS COUNTY, 102
HARRIS, GENE, 69
HARRISON MUSEUM OF AFRICAN-AMERICAN CULTURE, 42, 104
HARRISON, RICHARD, 44
HARSH VIVIAN COLLECTION OF AFRO-AMERICAN HISTORY AND LITERATURE, 69, 70
HARTFORD, CONNECTICUT, 130
HASTIE, WILLIAM HENRY ROOM, 100
HATCH-BILLOPS COLLECTION, 34, 86
HATHAWAY, ISAAC, 51
HAYDEN, PALMER, 52
HAWAII, 141
HAWKINS, CHARLOTTE EUGENIA, 89
HEALTH EDUACTION AND WELFARE DEPARTMENT, 98
HEARTMAN COLLECTION, 101
HELLO, DOLLY, 87

HEMPSTEAD, NEW YORK, 33, 119
HENDERSON, ERSKIN, 134
HENDERSON, MARK, 32
HENNING, TENNESSEE, 39, 100
HENSON, JOSIAH, REV., 129
HERITAGE HALL, 35
HERNDON HOME, 19, 65
HERNOON, ALONZO FRANKLIN, 65
HERZEL JUNIOR COLLEGE, 70
HESTER, GEORGIA, 23
HEWITT, MARY JANE, 14
HICKORY HILL, 134
HICKMAN, KENTUCKY, 23
HICKS, LOUIS C. 41
HIGH SCHOOL, 7
HILL DON COLLECTION, 63
HILLARY, ASA G. III.,127
HILLDALE BASEBALL CLUB OF DARBY PENNSYLVANIA, 95
HINDUISM, 72
HIPPOCRATES, 142
HISPANIC, 75
HISTORICAL SOCIETIES, 111
HITSVILLE, Y.S.A., 80
HOBSON CITY, ALABAMA, 141
HODGES, RUTH GALLERY, 20
HOFFMAN, MALVINIA COLLECTION, 70
HOGUE, GWENDOLYN HARKLESS, 79
HOLLYWOOD, CALIFORNIA, 80
HOLMES, CYNTHIA, 22
HONOLULU, HAWAII, 141
HOOD, EVELYN, 22
HOOKER, JOHN LEE, 133
HOPE SHIP, 79
HOSKINS, WILLIAM, 14
HOT HOUSE GALLERY, 21
HOUSE, SON, 133
HOUSTON PUBLIC LIBRARY, 122
HOUSTON, TEXAS, 41, 101, 102, 104, 114, 121
HOUSTON, WILLIE, 33
HOWARD COUNTY CENTER OF AFRICAN-AMERICAN CULTURE, 26
HOWARD UNIVERSITY, 16, 59, 64, 86, 142
HOWARD UNIVERSITY MUSEUM, 59
HOYTE, LENON H, 33
HUDSON, GLORIA J. GIBSON, 123
HUGHES, LANGSTON INSTITUTES, INC. CENTER FOR CULTURAL HISTORY AND ARTS ED., 33
HUNT, RICHARD, 84
HUNTER ABOLITION AND ANTI-SLAVERY COLLECTION, 121
HUNTINGTON, WEST VIRGINIA, 141
HUNTSVILLE A&M, 49

HUNTSVILLE, ALABAMA, 11
HURD, M. BABE, 134
HURSTON, ZORA NEALE MUSEUM OF ART, 17
HUSTON-TILLOTSON COLLEGE, 76, 103
HUTCHINSON, WILLIE C., 61

I

IBO, 135
IDAHO, XII, 21, 69
IDAHO BLACK HISTORY MUSEUM, 21, 69
IDAHO SPRINGS, COLORADO, 55
ILLINOIS, 21, 22, 69-74, 111 – 115, 120, 134, 141
ILLINOIS BLACK HISTORY, 134
ILLINIOS CENTRAL, 137
ILLINOIS STATE UNIVERSITY, 114
I LOVE NEW YORK HARLEM TRAVEL GUIDE, 88
INDEPENDENT ORDER OF ST. LUKE, 106
INDIANS, 55, 73
INDIANA, 22, 23, 74, 111, 122, 123, 123, 133, 141
INDIANA AFRICAN-AMERICAN HISTORICAL GENEALOGICAL SOCIETY, 111
INDIANA UNIVERSITY, 123
INDIANAPOLIS, INDIANA, 22, 23, 122, 124
INDIANAPOLIS PUBLIC SCHOOL SYSTEM, 74
INGLEWOOD, CALIFORNIA, 141
INTERNATIONAL BLACK HISTORY MUSEUM AND CULTURAL CENTER, 32
INTERNATIONAL COUNCIL OF MUSEUMS, 3
INSTITUTE OF MUSEUM AND LIBRARY SERVICES, 5
IOWA, 141
I.P. STANBACK MUSEUM AND PLANETARIUM, 6
IROQUOIS, 73
ISLAM, 72
ITHACA, NEW YORK, 117
ITURI FOREST PYGMIES, 70,

J

JACKSON, LILLIE CARROLL MUSEUM, INC. CIVIL RIGHTS MUSEUM, 26
JACKSON, MICHAEL, 80
JACKSON, MISSISSIPPI, 30, 83, 137
JACKSONVILLE, FLORIDA, 62, 120, 141
JACOBSON, DOROTHEA, 71
JACQUELINE HOUSE AFRICAN-AMERICAN MUSEUM, 30
JAMAICA, NEW YORK, 33
JAMAICA, 129
JAZZ, 77
JEFFERSON CITY, MISSOURI, 141

JEFFERSONVILLE, INDIANA, 133
JENKINS, DOROTHY, 62
JENKINS, JAME, S. T., 28, 80
JERSEY CITY, NEW JERSEY, 32, 85, 111, 118
JEWERLY, 6
JEWISH, 78
JOHANSON, DONALD, 4
JOHNSON BROTHERS, 123
JOHNSON, CLIFTON, 24
JOHNSON, GLENDORA, 33
JOHNSON, HELEN, 21
JOHNSON, HERSCHEL, 26
JOHNSON, IRENE, 17
JOHNSON, JAMES WELDON, 12
JOHNSON, JAMES WELDON COLLECTION OF CHILDREN'S BOOKS, 121
JOHNSON, LLOYD, 31
JOHNSON, LYNDON, 98
JOHNSON, OLA MAE, 116
JOHNSON OLA MAE BLACK HISTORICAL/MEMORABILIA SOCIETY, 117
JOHNSON PUBLISHING COMPANY, 120
JOHNSON, ROBERT, 133
JONES, ANN RUSSELL, 95
JONES, CASEY RAILROAD MUSEUM STATE PARK, 137
JONES, JOHNATHAN LUTHER CASEY, 137
JONES, OLIVER, 142
JOPLIN, SCOTT HOUSE, 31
JORDAN, ALMETTA, 31
JORDAY, BARBARA ARCHIVES, 101
JOURNAL OF AFRICAN CIVILIZATION AFRICANA STUDIES DEPARTMENT, 117
JOURNAL OF NEGRO HISTORY, 117
JUDAISM, 72
JULEE COTTAGE MUSEUM, 18
JUNEAU, ALASKA, 141
JUNIOR, PAMELA D.C., 30

K

KALAHARI BUSHMAN, 70
KAMBY BALONGO, 100
KANSAS, 23, 75, 116, 121, 141
KANSAS CITY JAZZ MUSEUM AND NEGRO LEAGUE BASEBALL MUSEUM, 31
KANSAS CITY, MISSOURI, 31, 84
KANSAS CITY PUBLIC LIBRARY, 121
KARAMU HOUSE, 91
KEALING PARK, 102
KECKLEY, ELIZABETH, 88
KENNEDY, JOHN FITZGERALD, 88
KENNEDY-KING COLLEGE, 72

KENNEDY, WINSTON, 16
KENT PUBLIC LIBRARY, 121
KENTE COLTH, 71
KENTUCKY, 23, 111, 133, 135, 142
KENTUCKY CENTER FOR AFRICAN-AMERICAN HERITAGE, 23
KENTUCKY DERBY MUSEUM, 133
KERR, BARBARA ANN, 75
KERR, DORIS, 75
KERR, LARKIN, 75
KEY WEST, FLORIDA, 18
KIAH, WILLIAM H., 77
KIMBALL, HELEN F., 89
KINARD, JOHN, 16
KING, CORETTA SCOTT, 64
KING, CURTIS, 40
KING, KENNEDY COLLEGE, 72
KING, MARTIN LUTHER JR., 69, 103
KING, MARTIN LUTHER JR. BRANCH, 121, 122
KING, MARTIN LUTHER JR. CENTER FOR NONVIOLENT SOCIAL CHANGE INC., 64
KING, MARTIN LUTHER MUSEUM OF BLACK CULTURE, 35
KING, MARTIN LUTHER JR. LIBRARY AND ARCHIVES, 19
KING, TISDELL COTTAGE, 67
KINTE, KUNTA, 100
KIZZY, 100
KLOTMAN PAVLUS R., 123
KNOXVILLE, TENNESSEE, 39, 100
KOENIG, ROBERT, 32
KRUIZE, PRISCILLA STEPHENS, 63
KUDJOE, OFUCTEY, 116
KU KLUX KLAN, 74, 143
KURTZ, MARIAN, 74
KWANZAA, 50
KYEREMATEN, A.A.Y., 71

L

LA AMISTAD, 76
LACY, LAURA J., 40
LANCASTER, CALIFORNIA, 13
LANE, RICHARD "NIGHT TRAIN," 82
LANEY, LUCY CRAFT MUSEUM OF BLACK HISTORY, 20, 65
LANGSTON, OKLAHOMA, 141
LAS VEGAS NEVADA, 31
LATIN AMERICAN, 84
LAW, W.W., VI
LAWNSIDE, NEW JERSEY, 116
LAWRENCE, GLACE W., 44
LEE, JOSEPH E., 120

LEE, ROBBIE E., 41
LEIGHTON, WILLIAM, 137
LE MOYNE-OWEN COLLEGE, 76
LERANSAW, DR., 20
LETTERS ON AMERICAN SLAVERY IN 1826, 136
LEVENWORTH, KANSAS, 23
LEVI COFFIN STATE HISTORIC SITE, 133
LEW, GERARD, 73
LEWIS AND BLALOCK COLLECTION, 117
LEWIS AND CLARK EXPEDITION, 69
LEWIS, GEORGE, 134
LEWIS, GERARD, 73
LEWIS, ISSAC, 134
LEWIS, OLIVER, 134
LEWIS, SAMELLA, DR., 52
LEWIS, STEVE, 117
LEWIS, WILLIAM III, 41
LEXINGTON, MISSISSIPPI, 30
LIBBERTY BELL, XIII
LBBERTY HILL HOME, 136
LIDDELL, PATRICIA, RESEARCHERS, CHICAGO CHAPTER AAHG'S, 113
LIFT EVERY VOICE AND SING = NEGRO NATIONAL ANTHEM, 145
LIGON, DORIS, 26
LINCOLN, ABRAHAM, 143
LINCOLN FOUNDATION, 134
LINCOLN HEIGHTS, OHIO, 141
LINCOLN, MARY TODD, 88
LINCOLN MEMORIAL CEMETARY, 143
LINN-HENLEY LIBRARY FOR SOUTHERN HISTORICAL RESEARCH, 119
LITTLE EGYPT CHAPTER AAHG, 112
LITTLE ROCK, ARKANSAS, 12
LIVING HISTORY PERFORMANCE GROUPS, 122
LIVINGSTONE COLLEGE, 35
LIZ, 100
LLOYD, TOM, 33
LONG ISLAND, 76
LOS ANGELES, CALIFORNIA, 13, 14, 51, 112, 115 – 120
LOS ANGELES CONSERVANCY 1999 PRESERVATION AWARY, 53
LOS ANGELES COUNTY PUBLIC LIBRARY, 118
LOS ANGELES PUBLIC LIBRARY, 119
LOUIS, JOE, 49, 82
LOUISIANA, 24, 25, 75, 76
LOUISIANA MUSEUM OF AFRICAN-AMERICAN HISTORY, 24
LOUISVILLE, KENTUCKY, 23, 111, 134
LOVE, JOSEPHINE HARRELD, 79
LOW COUNTY, 98
LOWE, ANN, 88
LUCY, 4
LUV LIFE COLLECTIBLES AND LIVING HISTORY MUSEUM, 11

M

MACK, THE KNIFE, 87
MACK, TOM, 16
MACON, GEORGIA, 20, 66
MADISON, GEORGIA, 20, 66
MADISON, INDIANA, 133
MAGDALEN SOCIETY, 131
MAINE, 115, 129
MAJOR CITIES WITHOUT AFRICAN-AMERICAN MUSEUMS, 141
MAJOR LEAGUE BASEBALL, 84
MAKEMBA, 79
MAKING THEIR MASK, 50
MAKONDE, 71, 72
MALCOLM "X", 5
MALCOLM COLLEGE, 22, 70, 71, 72
MADIGO, 100
MANATEE FAMILY HERITAGE HOUSE, 17
MANGBETU WOMEN, 71
MANN, CELIA, 96
MANN, SIMONS COTTAGE MUSEUM OF AFRICAN-AMERICAN CULTURE, 96
MANUSCRIPTS, 6
MAPS, 6
MARABASH MUSEUM, 32
MARDI GRAS INDIAN, 50
MARITIME, 6
MARQUENTE DOLEMAN HOUSE MUSEUM, 26
MARTIN, JO ANNE, 19
MARTIN, RITA, 35
MARYLAND, 25, 26, 76, 77, 113, 115, 118, 120
MARYLAND COLONIZATION SOCIETY, 132
MARYLAND MUSEUM OF AFRICAN ART, 26
MASAI, 79
MANSION, VAN LEW, 107
MASON CHAPEL AFRICAN A.M.E. CHURCH, 93
MASSACHUSETTS, 27, 28, 77
MASSACHUSETTS 54TH REGIMENT, 78
MAY COMPANY, 52
MAYNARD, JOHN 32
MAYS, BENJAMIM DR., 64
MCFARLANE, 62
MCCABE, V. THE ATCHISON TOPEKA AND SANTA FE RAILWAY COMPANY, 6
MCNEIL, ADRIENNE, 65
MEDICINE, 6, 142
MEETING HOUSE, 78
MEMPHIS, TENNESSEE, 6, 40, 49, 137
MEMPHIS BLUES, 49

MERIDIAN, MISSISSIPPI, 83, 141
MERRITT, CAROLE, 19
MESO-AMERICA, 102
METHODIST CHURCH CONFERENCE, 131
MGM/UA, 124
MEXICO, 103
MIAMI, FLORIDA, 17, 62, 63
MICHEAUX, OSCAR, 81, 123
MICHIGAN, 28, 29, 79, 113, 120, 122
MIDDLE PASSAGE, 130
MIDDLE TENNESSEE CONFERENCE AFRO-AMERICAN SCHOLARS, 115
MIDWAY, GEORGIA, 123
MILLER, ZELL, 66
MILLEDGEVILLE, GEORGIA, 67
MILWAUKEE, WISCONSIN, 42, 112, 123
MINE, 55
MINNEAPOLIS, MINNESOTA, 120, 141
MINNEAPOLIS, PUBLIC LIBRARY AND INFORMATION CENTER, 120
MINNESOTA, 120, 141
MISSISSIPPI, 30, 83, 137, 141
MISSISSIPPI DELTA, 133
MISSISSIPPI RIVER, 6
MISSOURI, 30, 31, 82, 84, 85, 121, 135, 141
MITCHELL, V. UNITED STATES, 6
MITCHELL, WILLIAM, 107
MOBILE, ALABAMA, 11, 119
MOBILE BLACK HISTORY MUSEUM, 11
MODEL CITY CULTURAL CENTER, 63
MOBILE PUBLIC LIBRARY, 119
MONROE COUNTY, 62
MONROE, GRACE, 114
MONROE, LOUISIANA, 24
MONTANA, 133
MONTGOMERY, ALABAMA, 114
MOONEY, NEIL C., 63
MOORE, COLLEGE OF ART, 95
MOORE, DAN, 19, 64
MOORE, HORACE, 66
MOORE, JUANITA, 40
MOORE, WILLIAM, 132
MOOREHEAD, LEEDELL-GRAHAM FINE ARTS GALLERY, 13, 51
MOOREHOUSE COLLEGE, 117
MOORLAND, JESSE E. COLLECTION, 59
MOORLAND-SPINGARN RESEARCH CENTER, 16, 59
MORGAN COUNTY AFRICAN-AMERICAN MUSEUM, 20, 66, 67
MORGAN STATE UNIVERSITY, 25, 15, 76
MORMONS, 69
MORRILL ACT, 6
MORSE, ANNIE RUTH, 39

MOSLER, AMORY KAY, 34
MOTHER BETHEL A.M.E. CHURCH, 37
MOTION PICTURES, 6
MOTOWN HISTORICAL MUSEUM, 28, 80
MOTOWN SOUND, 80
MOULTON, ELVINA, 69
MOUND BAYOU, MISSISSIPPI, 141
MOUSEION, 3
MOZAMBIQUE, 72
MUHAMMAD, ELIJAH, 46
MURALS, 72
MURPHY AFRICAN-AMERICAN MUSEUM, 12
MURPHY, ISAAC, 133
MURPHY, ROBERT, 93
MURRAY, ALFRED REV., 66
MUSEE, ROSETTE ROCHON, 24
MUSES, 3
MUSEUM OF AFRICAN-AMERICAN ART, 14, 19, 35, 52
MUSEUM OF AFRICAN-AMERICAN CULTURE MANNS SIMONS COTTAGE, 38, 96
MUSEUM OF AFRICAN-AMERICAN LIFE AND CUTLURE, 40, 103, 104
MUSEUM OF AFRICAN AND AFRO-AMERICAN ART AND ANTIQUITIES, 33
MUSEUM OF AFRIKAN-AMERICAN HISTORY – FLINT, 29
MUSEUM OF AFRO-AMERICAN HISTORY, 27, 78
MUSEUM OF BLACK INVENTORS, 125
MUSEUM OF THE NATIONAL CENTEROF AFRO-AMERICAN ARTISTS, 27
MUSICAL INSTRUMENTS, 6
MYERES, CAROLYN J., 75

N

NAACP, 68, 85, 134
NAACP/HENRY LEE MOON LIBRABY AND NATIONAL CIVIL RIGHTS ARCHIVES, 26
NAACP HISTORICAL AND CULTURAL PROJECT, 118
NACOTCHTANK INDIANS, 56
NAIROBE, KENYA, 71
NANTUCKET, MASSACHUSETTS, 27
NASHVILLE, TENNESSEE, 40, 115
NATCHEZ, MISSISSIPPI, 30
NATCHEZ MUSEUM OF AFRO-AMERICAN HISTORY, 30
NATIONAL AFRICAN-AMERICAN ARCHIVES, 11
NATIONAL AFRICAN-AMERICAN ARCHIVES AND MUSEUM, 11
NATIONAL AFRO-AMERICAN MUSEUM AND CULTURAL CENTER, 36, 94
NATIONAL AFRO-AMERICAN SPORTS HALL OF FAME AND GALLERY, 29, 82
NATIONAL ARTS OF TAZANIA, 72
NATIONAL BLACK MEMORABILIA COLLECTION ASSOCIATION, 118
NATIONAL CENTER FOR AFRO-AMERICAN ARTISTS, 27
NATIONAL CIVIL RIGHTS MUSEUM, 6
NATIONAL CIVIL RIGHTS MUSEUM/LORRAINE CIVIL RIGHTS MUSEUM, 40

NATIONAL COUNCIL FOR EDUCATION AND ECONOMIC DEVELOPMENT, 17
NATIONAL COUNCIL OF NEGRO WOMEN, 57
NATIONAL CAPITOL AREA CHAPTER AAHG, 113
NATIONAL CONFERENCE OF NEGRO ARTIST, 71
NATIONAL CONFERENCE OF STATE MUSEUM ASSOCIATION, 5
NATIONAL MUSEUM OF AFRICAN ART SMITHSONIAN INSTITUTE, 16, 59, 60
NATIONAL MUSEUM OF AFRO-AMERICAN HISTORY, 30
NATIONAL MUSEUM OF THE TUSKEGEE AIRMAN, 29
NATIONAL NEGRO MUSEUM AND HISTORICAL FOUNDATION, 73
NATIONAL PARK SERVICE, 56, 57, 87, 106
NATIONAL UNDERGROUND RAILROAD MUSEUM, 23
NATIVE AMERICANS, 76
NEBRASKA, 31
NEGRO, 5, 142
NEGRO CIVIL CLUB, 61
NEGRO HISTORY WEEK, 143
NEGRO LEAGUE, 95
NEGRO LEAGUES BASEBALL MUSEUM, 84, 85
NEGRO PUBLIC LIBRARY, 132
NEGRO SOCIETY FOR HISTORICAL RESEARCH, 88
NESQUEHONING, PENNSYLVANIA, 131
NEVADA, 31, 141
NEWARK, NEW JERSEY, 32, 118, 120
NEWARK PUBLIC LIBRARY, 121
NEW BRUNSWICK, NEW JERSEY, 117
NEW CANTON, VIRGINIA, 142
NEW ENGLAND, 78, 89
NEW HAVEN CONNECTICUT, 15, 55, 111, 141
NEW JERSEY, 32, 85, 111, 113, 116, 116, 120
NEW JERSEY CHAPTER AAHG, 113
NEW JERSEY CITY, NEW JERSEY, 85
NEW MUSE COMMUNITYMUSEUM OF BOOKLYN, 32
NEW ORLEANS AFRICAN-AMERICAN MUSEUM, 23
NEW ORLEANS, LOUISIANA, 24, 75, 76
NEWSPAPERS, 6
NEW YORK, 6, 32, 33, 34, 35, 85, 111, 112, 113, 115 – 120, 124
NEW YORK CITY, NEW YORK, 49, 67, 68, 76, 87, 88, 119, 120, 124, 131
NILE RIVER, 4, 142
NOBLE HILL WHEELER MEMORIAL CENTER, 65, 66
NOBLE HILL BLACK HISTORY MUSEUM, 23
NORMA MOTION PICTURE COLLECTION,124
NORMAL, ALABAMA, 12, 49
NORMAL, ILLINOIS, 114
NORMAN, GEORGETTE M., 11
NORTH AMERICAN, XII
NORTH AMERICAN BLACK HISTORICAL MUSEUM AND CULTURAL CENTER, 44
NORTH BUXTON, CANADA, 44
NORTH CAROLINA, 35, 89, 113, 135, 141
NORTH CAROLINA AAHG, 113

NORTH CAROLINA CENTRAL UNIVERSITY MUSEUM OF ART, 35
NORTH CAROLINA QUAKERS, 133
NORTHERN CALIFORNIA CENTER FOR AFRO-AMERICAN HISTORY, 14, 53
NORTH STAR, 133
NOVA SCOTIA, CANADA, 45
NTU ART ASSOCIATION KIRKPATRICK CENTER, 37
NUAMAH, ALBERT AND BREANDA, 28
NUER WARRIOR, 71
NUGENT, BRUCE, 86

O

OAKLAND, CALIFORNIA, 14, 53, 119
OAKLAND PUBLIC LIBRARY, 119
OHIO, 36, 37, 91–94, 112, 113, 120, 133, 136, 141
OHIO RIVER, 129, 136
OHIO SLAVE HOUSE, 134
OKLAHOMA, 37, 141
OKLAHOMA CITY, OKLAHOMA, 37
OLD DILLARD HIGH SCHOOL MUSEUM, 17, 61
OLD SCHOOL BUILDING, XII
OLD SHAWNEETOWN, 134
OLD STENTORIAN, 53
OLD WASHINGTON, ARKANSAS, 13
OLIN, JIM, 105
OMAHA, NEBRASKA, 31
ONASSIS, JACQUELINE KENNEDY, 88
O'NEAL, TOILYNN, 36
ONEIDA, 73
ONTARIO BLACK HISTORY SOCIETY, 44
OPA LOCKA, FLORIDA, 62
OPEN HAND PUBLISHER, 117
OPHER, MOSES, 77
OPPORTUNITIES INDUSTRIAL CENTER, 96
ORANGEBURG, SOUTH CAROLINA, 97
ORCHARD STREET CULTURAL MUSEUM, 26
ORDINNANCE OF 1787, 136
OREGON, 141
ORLANDO, FLORIDA, 18
OSKALOOSA COUNTY SCHOOL BOARD, 61
OVERTOWN COMMUNITY, 62
OWENS, ANDI, 33
OWENS, JIMMY, 86
OXON HILL, MARYLAND, 120
OZARK COUNTY, 50
OZARKS AFRO-AMERICAN HERITAGE MUSEUM, 30

P

PAAYA PA GALLERY, 71
PACHAI, BIRDGLAL, 45
PACIFIC ISLANDS, 102
PACIFIC OCEAN, 71
PADUCAH, KENTUCKY, 141
PAINTINGS, 6
PALM BEACH COUNTY, 62
PALMER, ALICE FREEMAN, 89
PALMER, CYNTHIA, 100
PALMER HOUSE, 100
PALMER MEMORIAL INSTITUTE, 89
PALMER, WILL E., 100
PANOPLY OF GHANA, 71
PAPER SCULPTURE, 6
PARAMOUNT PICTURES, 124
PARKER-GRAY ALUMNI ASSOCIATION, 106
PARKER, HENRY, 55
PARKER, NINA, G., 36, 93
PARKS, ROSA, 88
PARKS, ROSA LIBRARY AND MUSEUM, 11
PASQUINE, RUTH, 13
PATERSON, HENRY, C., 132
PARTING WAYS: MUSEUM OF AFRO-AMERICAN ETHNIC HISTORY, INC., 27
PATTON, CHARLIE, 133
PEESKILL, NEW YORK, 112
PENDELTON FOUNDATION FOR BLACK HISTORY AND CULTURE, 39
PENDELTON, SOUTH CAROLINA, 39
PENDERGRAFT, NORMAN, 35
PENN CENTER FOREMORE PLANTATION, 39
PENNSYLVANIA, 37, 94, 95, 113, 123, 131, 141
PENSACOLA, FLORIDA, 18
PEORIA, ILLINOIS, 22
PERKINS, JAMES "SOUP", 133
PERRIS, CALIFORNIA, 14
PERSONAL PROPERTY, XII
PETERSBURG, VIRGINIA, 105, 141
PETERSON, EVA F., 36
PETERSON, HORACE III, 31
PHILADELPHIA DOLL MUSEUM, 6, 38, 95
PHILADELPHIA FELLOWSHIP COMMISSION, 131
PHILADELPHIA, PENNSYLVANIA, 37, 94, 95,113, 122, 123, 131
PHILLIPS, DUNNING-BURGESS SCHOOL, 5
PHILLIPS, WENDELL, 69, 68
PHONEIX, ARIZONA, 12, 112, 141
PHOENIX BANK OF NANSEMON, 42
PHOTOGRAPHS, 6

PIEDMONT, 89
PIEDMONT COLLEGE, 76
PINE BLUFF, ARKANSAS, 13, 51
PIONEERS, 5
PITTSBURGH, PENNSYLVANIA, 141
PLANETARIUM, 97
PLEDGE TO THE RED, BLACK AND GREEN, 144
PLESSY V. FERGUSON, 6
PLUS, 100
PLYMOUTH, MASSACHUSETTS, 27
POLICE DEPARTMENT, 131
PORTLAND, OREGON, 141
PORTLAND, MAINE, 115
PORTUGUESE, 142
POSS HOMES HIGH RISE, 98
POSTON, ROGER, 38
POTTAWATIOMI, 73
POWELL, ADAM CLAYTON JR. MUSEUM, 33
POWELL, GEORGETTE, 16
PRESBYTERIAN, 136
PRICE, LOUIS, 55
PRICHARD, ALABAMA, 119
PRICHARD MEMORIAL LIBRARY, 119
PRINCE GEORGE'S COUNTY MEMORIAL LIBRARY SYSTEM, 120
PRINTS, 6
PROSCENIUM THEATRE, 91
PROVIDENCE, RHODE ISLAND, 38, 95
PUCE, CANADA, 44
PUERTO RICANS, 75
PULITZER, PRIZE, 100
PULLMAN, PHILLIP RANDOLPH PORTER MUSEUM 21
PYRAMID, 142

Q

QUEENS COLLEGE CUNY, 87, 116
QUEENS, NEW YORK, 34
QUINCY CLUB, 73

R

RACINE, WISCONSIN, 141
RADIO, 6
RALEIGH, NORTH CAROLINA, 112, 141
RANDOLPH, WILMA, 82
RANKIN HOUSE, 136
RANKIN, JEAN, 136

RANKIN, JOHN REV., 129, 136
RAY, ERNESTINE, 17
READING, PENNSYLVANIA, 38
REDDY, KRISHMA, 86
REED, ERLENE, 15
REED, MATTYE AFRICAN HERITAGE CENTER, 35
RENO, NEVADA, 141
REVOLUTIONARIES, 5
REVOLUTIONARY WAR, 137
REYNOLDS, EARL, 105
RHODE ISLAND, 38, 95, 96
RHODE ISLAND BLACK HERITAGE SOCIETY, 38, 95
RICH HERITAGE ANDA CONTINUING LEGACY, 50
RICHLAND COUNTY HISTORIC PRESERVATION COMMISSION, 96
RICHMOND, DON G., 24
RICHMOND HEIGHTS, FLORIDA, 62
RICHMOND, VIRGINIA, 42, 106
RICKEY, BRANCH, 84
RIPLEY, OHIO, 136
RIPLEY, S. DILLION, 56
RIVER ROAD AFRICAN-AMERICAN MUSEUM 24
ROANOKE VALLEY, 105
ROANOKE, VIRGINIA, 42, 104
ROBBINS HISTORICAL SOCIETY, 111
ROBBINS, ILLINOIS, 111, 141
ROBBINS, WARREN M., 59
ROBERTSON SMITH BLACK CULTURAL CENTER, 30, 83
ROBINSON, JACKIE, 84, 85
ROBINSON, SUGAR RAY, 82
ROCHESTER, NEW YORK, 34
ROCK COMMUNITY IMPROVEMENT LEAGUE, 77
ROCKFORD, ILLINOIS, 141
ROCK ISLAND/MOLINE, ILLINOIS, 141
RODDY, BERTHA MAXWELL DR., 90
ROLLA, LENDRA, 41
ROME, NEW YORK, 4, 115
ROOTS, 100
ROSENWALD FOUNDATION, 70
ROXBURY, 78
RUNTAGH, EUGENE, REV. PAPERS, 131
RUTGERS UNIVERSITY, 117

S

SACRAMENTO, CALIFORNIA, 141
SAHARA DESERT, 59, 60, 71, 142
ST. AUGUSTINE, FLORIDA, 62
ST. HELENA ISLAND, SOUTH CAROLINA, 39

ST. JOHN RIVER, 97
ST. LOUIS, MISSOURI, 31, 83, 84
ST. LOUIS BLUES, 49
ST. LOUIS PUBLIC LIBRARY, 121
ST. LUKE HERALD NEWSPAPER, 107
ST. LUKE PENNY SAVINGS BANK, 106
ST. MARY'S GREEK CATHOLIC CHURCH, 131
ST. MARTIN ARCHANGEL CHURCH, 131
ST. PAUL BAPTIST, 69
ST. PETER CLAVER CHURCH, 132
SALINE RIVER VALLEY, 134
SANDUSKY OHIO, 80
SAN ANGELO, TEXAS, 129
SAN ANTONIO, TEXAS, 41
SAN DIEGO, CALIFORNIA, 14
SAN FRANCISCO AFRICAN-AMERICAN HISTORICAL AND CUTLURAL SOCIETY, INC. 14, 54
SAN FRANCISCO, CALIFORNIA, 14, 54, 118
SAN JOSE, CALIFORNIA, 141
SAN JUAN, PUERTO RICO, 88
SANDERS, GERALD, 22
SANDS, LOFTON B. AFRICAN BAHAMAS MUSEUM, 18
SANKOFA, 49
SARA GIRL, 71
SATCHMO, 87
SAUNDERS, MALINDA, 118
SAUNDERS, WALLACE, 137
SAVANNAH, GEORGIA, VI, 6, 20, 67, 68, 137
SAVANNAH HISTORY MUSEUM, 137
SAVANNAH STATE UNIVERSITY, 68
SCHOMBURG CENTER FOR RESEARCH IN BLACK CULTURE, 34, 88
SCIENCES, 3, 6
SCIENTIFIC AMERICAN MAGAZINE, 67, 68
SCOT, JEAN SAMPSON GREATER NEW YORK CHAPTER AAHG'S, 113
SCOTT, J. RUPERT, 16
SEABROOK VILLAGE FOUNDATION, 123
SEATTLE, WASHINGTON, 42, 112, 117, 122,
SEATTLE PUBLIC LIBRARY, 122
SECONDARY CITIES THAT NEED AFRICAN-AMERICAN MUSEUMS, 141
SEDALIA, NORTH CAROLINA, 35, 89
SEMNG PYGMY MALAYSIA, 71
SHABAZZ, 71
SHELTON, DELORES, 64
SHELLEY V. KRAMER, 6
SHEPPARD, WILLIAM H. DR., 105
SHILOH BAPTIST CHURCH, 143
SIMMONS COLLECTION AFRICAN ARTS MUSEUM, 85, 86
SIMMONS, STANDFIELD, 32, 86
SIMONS, AGNES JACKSON, 96
SIMONS, BILL, 96

SIMONS, CHARLES, 96
SIMPSON'S COLLECTION AT WADSWORTH ATHENEUM, 130
SLAVE CABIN MUSEUM, 99
SLAVE FORT, 6
SLAVE HAVEN/UNDERGROUND RAILROAD, 137
SLAVE QUARTERS, XII
SMA AFRICAN ARTS MUSEUM, 32
SMITH, DOLPHUS L. REV., 93
SMITH, GREER, 32
SMITH V. ALLWRIGHT, 6
SMITHSONIAN INSTITUTION, 56, 59
SOCIETY FOR PRESERVATION OF WEEKSVILLE AND BEDFORD STUYVESANT HISTORY, 32
SOCIETY FOR THE PRESERVATION OF BLACK HERTIAGE, 106
SOJOURNER TRUTH ROOM, 120
SOLOMON ISLANDER, 70
SOUTH AFRICA, 71
SOUTH AMERICA, 52, 104
SOUTH BEND, INDIANA, 141
SOUTH CAROLINA, 38, 96, 97, 98, 116
SOUTH CAROLINA STATE COLLEGE, 6, 97
SOUTH CAROLINA VOLUNTEER INFANTRY, 137
SOUTH DALLAS CULTURAL CENTER, 40
SOUTH END, 78
SOUTH PACIFIC, 52
SOUTHSIDE COMMUNITY ART CENTER, 22
SPAIN, 73
SPANISH, 53, 72
SPINGARN, ARTHUR B. COLLECTION, 59
SPIRIT OF FREEDOM FOUNDATION, 83
SPRINGFIELD, ILLINOIS, 141
SPRINGFIELD, MASSACHUSETTS, 27
SPOKANE, WASHINGTON, 141
STAGVILLE CENTER, 135, 136
STAMPS, 6
STANBACK, I.P. MUSEUM AND PLANETARIUM SOUTH CAROLINA STATE COLLEGE, 97
STANLEY, EZEKIEL, 77
STANLEY INSTITUTE AND CHRIST ROCK, 26, 76, 77
STATE BLACK ARCHIVES RESEARCH CENTER AND MUSEUM, 49, 50
STEAMSHIP PASSENGER LISTS, 131
STEARNS, NORMAN "TURKEY", 82
STEMANS, JAMES S., 132
STEPHENS AFRICAN AMERICAN MUSEUM, 25
STEWART, MARIA W., 78
STEWART, PAUL C., 55
STEWART, ROWENA, 37
STILES AFRICAN-AMERICAN HERITAGE CENTER, 15
STILES, GRACE, 15
STILL FAMILY HISTORICAL COMMITTEE, 116
STOKEES, CAROL, 92

STONE, CARRIE, 89
STONE, GALEN, 89
STORE FRONT MUSEUM/PAUL ROBERSON THEATRE, 33
STOVALL JENNELLE, 22
STOVALL, MELODY, 42
STOWE, HARRIET BEECHER, 136
STOWE, HARRIET BEECHER HOUSE & MUSEUM, 129
STUDIO MUSEUM IN HARLEM, 34
SUFFOLK, VIRGINIA, 42
SUDAN, 60
SUDAN WOMAN, 71
SUITLAND, MARYLAND, 143
SULLIVANS ISLAND, SOUTH CAROLINA, 39
SUMMER, CHARLES, 78
SWAHILI, 91
SWEAT V. PLAINER, 6
SWISHER, CAROL LIBRARY/LEARNING RESOURCE CENTER, 17
SYRACUSE, NEW YORK, 34

T

TACOMA, WASHINGTON, 42
TAKEI, GEORGE, 86
TALBOT COUNTY, MARYLAND, 58
TALLADEGA COLLEGE, 76
TALLAHASSEE, FLORIDA, 18, 63
TAMPA, FLORIDA, 19
TANZANIA, AFRICA, 71, 72, 142
TAOISM, 72
TAPPAN, LEWIS, 76
TARRANT COUNTY BLACK HISTORICAL AND GENEALOGICAL SOCIETY, INC., 41, 112
TATUM ART CULTURAL CENTER, 121
TAYLOR, GILBERT L., 74
TAYLOR, THOMAS, 85
TEASLEY, RON, 82
TECHNOLOGICAL, 6
TEIXERIRA, JOAQUINA BELA, 38
TELEVISION, 6
TENAFLY, NEW JERSEY, 32
TENNESSEE, 39, 69, 98, 99, 100, 115, 137
TENNESSEE STATE UNIVERSITY, 115
TERRY, ROBIN, 28
TEXARKANA, TEXAS, 141
TEXAS, 40, 101 - 104, 112, 114, 122, 129, 141
TEAXS CENTENNIAL EXPOSITION, 104
TEXAS SOUTHERN UNIVERSITY, 41, 101, 102
TEXAS STATE CHAPTER AAHGS, 114
TEXTBOOKS, 7

TEXTILES, 6
319 GALLERY, 34
THOMAS BOOKER, FANNIE, 30
THOMAS, INGRID, 122
THOMAS, PHILLIP, 118
THOMAS, WARREN BLACK MUSEUM, 23
THOMPSON, ANDERSON DR., 116
THOMPSON, DOROTHY AFRICAN-AMERICAN MUSEUM, 17
THOMPSON, HAZEL, 105
THOMPSON-HICKMAN LIBRARY, 133
THOMPSON, LLOYD, 95
THURMAN, HOWARD, 54
TIBBS-EVANS COLLETION, 16
TIBBS, THURLOW E. JR., 16, 58
TILL, 100
TISDELL-KING COTTAGE, 20, 67
TOLEDO, OHIO, 121
TOMORROW'S WORLD ART CENTER, 16
TOOLS, 6
TOLEDO, OHIO 121
TOPEKA, KANSAS, 116, 141
TORNOTO, CANADA, 44
TOTAL ACTION AGAINST POVERTY, 104
TOUGALOO COLLEGE, 76
TOUGALOO COLLEGE ART MUSEUM, 30
TOUGALOO, MISSISSIPPI, 30
TOWERS MARY WALKER, 98
TOYS, 6
TRAVELING MUSEUMS, 124
TREASURE HOUSE BRANCH, 92
TROLLEY THEATER, 64
TRUTH, SOJOURNER, 71
TUBMAN, HARRIET, 63
TUBMAN, HARRIET GALLERY, 27
TUBMAN, HARRIET ASSOCIATION OF DORCHESTER, 115
TUBMAN. HARRIET HISTORICAL AND CULTURAL MUSEUM, 20, 66
TUBMAN, HARRIET MUSEUM AND CULTURAL ASSOCIATION, 36
TUCSON, ARIZONA, 141
TULLANE UNIVERSITY, 24
TULSA, OKLAHOMA, 141
TURNER, GWEN, 12
TURNER, PAUL, 64
TURNER, RALPH, 73
TUSCALOOSA, ALABAMA, 12
TUSKEGEE, ALABAMA, 12
TUSKEGEE INSTITUTE, 130
TUSKEGEE INSTITUTE NATIONAL HISTORIC SITE, 12
TYLER, TEXAS, 131
TYSON, CECILY, 64

U

UBANGI WOMAN, 71
UCLA CENTER FOR AFRO-AMERICAN STUDIES, 117
UNCLE BOB'S ROOM, 135
UNCLE REMUS MUSEUM, 129
UNCLE TOM'S CABIN HISTORICAL SITE #40, 45, 129, 133
UNDERGROUND RAILROAD, 34, 129, 136, 137
UNICAL UNIVERSITY INTELLIGENCE COSMIC AWARENESS, 118
UNION SPRING, ALABAMA, 98
UNITED NATIONS, 71
UNITED NEGRO COLLEGE FUND, 132
UNITED STATES, 52, 72, 74, 94, 103, 104, 105
UNITED STATES SUPREME COURT, 76
UNITED SOUTH END SETTLEMENT, 27
UNIVERSITY MUSEUM HAMPTON UNIVERSITY, 105
UNIVERSITY OF CALIFORNIA AT LOS ANGELES, 116
UNIVERSITY OF CHICAGO, 142
UNIVERSITY OF THE DISTRICT OF COLUMBIA, 124
UPPER MARLBORO, MARYLAND, 118
UTAH, 69

V

VALHALAHA, NEW YORK, 35
VAUGHN CULTURAL CENTER, 31, 83
VAUGHN, ERMALENE, 83
VAUGHAN, MISSISSIPPI, 137
VICKSBURG AFRO-AMERICAN MUSEUM/STUDIO, INC., 30
VICKSBURG, MISSISSIPPI, 30
VILLAGE OF JUFFURE, 100
VINEY, 100
VIRGINIA, 41, 104 – 107, 141, 142
VIRGINIA CITY, MONTANA, 133
VIRGIN ISLANDS, 100

W

WADDELL GALLERY, 20
WADSWORTH ATHENEUM, 130
WAGE EARNERS SAVINGS AND LOAN BANK, 68
WAHAB, HANIF, 36
WALDORF, MARYLAND, 26
WALKER AFRICAN-AMERICAN MUSEUM AND RESEARCH CENTER, 31
WALKER HIRAM HISTORICAL MUSEUM, 44

WALKER, MADAME C.J., 121
WALKER, MADAME C.J. MUSEUM AND AFRO-AMERICAN CULTURAL FOUNDATION, 35
WALKER, MAGGIE NATIONAL HISTORICAL SITE, 106
WALKER, MARY HISTORICAL AND EDUCATIONAL FOUNDATION, 39, 98
WALKER, WILLIAM, 133
WALL OF RESPECT, 72
WALLS, JOHN FREEMAN HISTORIC SITE, 44
WALTON COUNTY GEORGIA, 65
WALTON COUNTY SCHOOL BOARD, 61
WANTAGE, NEW JERSEY, 113
WARLEY, BASCOM AND SONS, 132
WARNER BROTHERS, 124
WARNER JOSEPH, 42
WASHINGTON, 112, 117, 122, 141
WASHINGTON AUGUSTUS, 130
WASHINGTON, BOOKER T. MIDDLE SCHOOL, 62
WASHINGTON, BOOKER T. 130
WASHINGTON COUNTY, 77
WASHINGTON, D.C., (SEE DISTRICT OF COLUMBIA)
WASHINGTON, SAMUEL LEE, 82
WATERS, MUDDY, 133
WATKINS ACADEMY MUSEUM OF CULTURAL ARTS, 36
WATKINS, BRUCE R. CULTURAL HERITAGE CENTER, 31, 84
WATUSI, 70
WAX, 6
WAYNE COUNTY BUILDING, 29
WEAPONS, 6
WEBSTER DICTIONARY, 3, 80
WEBSTER, ISABEL GATES, 64
WELCH MORGAN, BEVERLY, A., 27
WELL'S BUILT MUSEUM OF AFRICAN-AMERICAN HISTORY, 18
WELLS, EARL, DR., 63
WELLESLEY COLLEGE, 89
WERER, 135
WESLEY, CHARLES, 5
WESTCHESTER AFRICAN-AMERICAN HISTORICAL SOCIETY, 34, 112
WESTCHESTER COMMUNITY COLLEGE, 35
WESTERN CIVILIZATION, 4
WESTERN RESERVE HISTORICIAL SOCIETY LIBRARY, 91
WEST INDIES , 104
WEST VIRGINIA, 141
WETUMPKA, ALABAMA, 12, 50
WHEELER, JAMES, 81
WHITE PLAINES, NEW YORK, 119
WHITE SPRINGS, FLORIDA, 19
WHITEMAN, BARBARA A., 38, 95
WHITTAKER, GALLERY, 97
WICHITA, KANSAS, 75
WILBERFORCE, OHIO, 36, 94

WILLIAM, A. JOHN, 86
WILLIAMS, DANIEL A., DR., 103
WILLIAMS, DANIEL HALE, 6
WILLIAMS, FRED HART GENEALOGICAL SOCEITY, 113
WILLIAMS HERBERT, 34
WILLIAMS, KATHRYN, 29
WILLIAMS, MARSHALL, 82
WILLIAMS, SYLVIA, 16
WILLIAMS, WALTER, 21
WILLINGBOARD, NEW JERSEY, 32
WILMINGTON, DELAWARE, 15, 111
WILSON, CURTIS, 36
WILSON, JAMES H. BUILDING, 50
WILSON, MARY L. NATIONAL HISTORIC SITE, 42
WILSON, MIRIAM B. FOUNDATION/OLD SLAVE MART, 39
WINDSOR, CANADA, 44
WINKFIELD, JAMES, 133
WINSTON/SALEM, NORTH CAROLINA, 141
WICHITA, KANSAS, 141
WRIGHT, CHARLES H. MUSEUM OF AFRICAN-AMERICAN HISTORY, 29
WISCONSIN, 42, 112, 122, 141
WISCONSIN BLACK HISTORICAL SOCIETY/MUSEUM, 42, 112
WITTER, ROBERT, 71
WIZ, 88
WOLF, HOWLIN, 133
WOLOG, 135
WOMEN'S RIGHTS, 58
WOOD, 6
WOODSON, ANNE ELIZA (RIDDLE), 142
WOODSON, CARTER, G., XII, 5, 73
WOODSON, CARTER, G. CENTER, 16, 114
WOODSON, CARTER G., FOUNDATION, 118
WOODSON, CARTER G. HISTORIAN, 142, 143
WOODSON, CARTER G., REGIONAL LIBRARY, 69, 70, 72, 120
WOODSON, JAMES HENRY, 142
WORKS PROGRESS ADMINISTRATION, 131, 132
WORLD SERIES, 84, 85
WORLD WAR II, 53, 73 137

Y

YATES AND MITLON DRUG STORE, 64
YMCA, 73
YMI CULTURAL CENTER, 35, 90
YORK, 69
YORK, PENNSYLVANIA, 38, 141
YOUNG, JAMES A. III, 20
YOUNGSTOWN, OHIO, 37, 141

YOUR HERITAGE HOUSE, 29, 79
YWCA, 72

Z

ZAIRE, 71
ZEIDLER, JEANNE, 42
ZULU, 79
ZULU WOMAN, 71